MW00658293

GOLD

is where it

FINDS YOU

The only survivor of a gold mining family shares their awe-inspiring journey.

Brian Johnson

GOLD
is where it
FINDS YOU

Published by
Fig Factor Media, LLC | www.figfactormedia.com
Cover Design & Layout by Juan Pablo Ruiz

Printed in the United States of America

ISBN: 978-1-959989-85-1

FIG
FACTOR
MEDIA

This book is dedicated to Linda,
the genuine gold in my life,
My daughter, Kelsey,
My wonderful parents, the late
Carroll and Phyllis Johnson,
and my brother, Loren, and
Delores Johnson.

TABLE OF CONTENTS

ACKNOWLEDGMENTS

I will begin by thanking my wife, Linda, the most incredible gold nugget I've found in my forty years of treasure hunting. This beautiful woman has stayed with me through the good and the difficult years. Thank you, Linda, for your many sacrifices in life to allow me to live my dream.

Looking back on the beginning of my adventurous life, I must acknowledge Roger, Lois, Douglas, and Timothy Green. The Greens opened the door to the possibility of my family's adventure by first being courageous enough to start their own mining venture in 1979. They then encouraged my family to do the same in 1981 and mentored us through it. Entering the world of gold mining was life-changing for the Johnsons, and Tim has kept me in it by welcoming me into his camp in Candle, Alaska, for which I am forever grateful.

I would also be negligent not to mention the mining community in Fairbanks, Alaska, and Whitehorse, Yukon, who helped create the many experiences shared in this book. Miners form tight-knit communities and regularly help each other in any way possible.

I also want to acknowledge the many supportive businesses in the nearby towns I mention throughout the book, many of which are still in operation today. We worked with some very extraordinary, caring people in both Fairbanks and Whitehorse, who understood the challenges facing miners in remote areas and did their best to make our experiences positive ones.

I want to thank Jacqueline Ruiz of Fig Factor Media for our four-hour breakfast that began the process of bringing this book to life. Without you, this book would still be a dream on the shelf. Thank you for believing in me. Your life and accomplishments continue to inspire me.

Juan Pablo Ruiz, thank you for this book's graphic design and layout. Your creative ability piques curiosity of what could lie within the pages of this book and generates positive reactions from those interested in reading it.

I also want to acknowledge Karen Dix for her time and effort in challenging me and my memory to create and accomplish this work. We have traveled together to Alaska and Yukon through our time together. You are now a gold miner in your own right with an authentic understanding of the life they lead. It has been a pleasure working with you.

INTRODUCTION

At an early age, I was fascinated by the history of the gold rush in California, Alaska, and the Yukon. I read books about it in school, never imagining that I would be experiencing a gold rush firsthand at the age of twenty-six. Little did I know that the price of gold would spike to $800 an ounce in 1980, and many hearty, adventurous hopefuls would head to the hills to make their fortune, just as many had done hundreds of years ago.

Twenty-one years ago, a friend of mine named Teresa Taylor Renfree, encouraged me to write this book after I shared a few of my stories from my days as a modern-day goldminer. Life was hectic, and I never thought it would happen. Then came COVID. I spent the lockdown in paradise, at my home in Puerto Vallarta, and it seemed like the perfect time to start writing. At first, I doubted I could remember enough details or write a book others would find interesting to read. However, the more I wrote, the more adventures came back to me. I remembered my childhood, how my parents raised me, and why those special thirty-five years spent mining with my parents and my brother, Loren, were the best years of my life.

Now, I am the sole survivor, the only one left to tell the story of our mining operation. I felt I must record our lives for the sake of my family and the next generation, but also for other mining families and all families who work alongside each other toward a dream.

As you embark on the mining adventure within these pages, be aware that I'm not sugarcoating any of my experiences. Placer gold mining is a complex and risky business. We have seen miners come and go, with wild success and heartbreaking failure. Camp life in a remote area can have life-threatening challenges, from the resident wildlife to trying to get along with your neighbors and even those in camp. I touch upon them in this book, but those experiences could fill another book alone.

My gold mining adventures are authentic, so they necessarily vary from the unrealistic, fictional drama you've seen on "reality" TV. Mine is the true story of a family that set out on a big adventure together in the gold fields of Alaska and the Yukon and found so much more than they were searching for.

Finally, I end this book with an important epilogue to encapsulate the lessons I have learned from my life. I believe we all have a purpose on Earth, and working to fulfill it results in wisdom. It has been especially true for me.

I hope you enjoy a glimpse into the life of my ordinary family doing not-so-ordinary things. Enjoy the adventure, and I sincerely hope you find the "gold" in your life, whatever it may be!

CHAPTER 1

TWO BOYS IN POPLAR

I've always believed life should be an adventure. I just never knew how big an adventure it could be.

I had a humble start in a simple town. If you head as far north as you can go in Wisconsin, almost to the shores of Lake Superior, you will hit Douglas County. And in that county, you will find my hometown of Poplar. Today about one thousand people live there. It was smaller in my childhood, but it was our world.

Poplar was, and still is, a friendly town with a bank, grocery store, café, post office, lumber yard, and, the most significant place to our family, Poplar Hardware. People could get almost any tool or home improvement necessity from the store without driving eighteen miles west to Superior, Wisconsin. We were regulars and soon became close friends with the Lundberg family, who owned the store. Later, Mom worked there as a bookkeeper. Many times, the high school teachers would drop in with a less than flattering report for her about her son, Brian, since I always gave them something to report.

I was born March 2, 1955, but my parents settled in what would become our family home when I was five. The old house sat along US Highway 2, a busy east-west highway that ran coast to coast. I hope my childhood homestead is still known as "the old Johnson place." There were five children in the family: my brother Lowell, followed by Karen, Loren, me, and Brenda. I was closest to Loren, who was twenty months older than me. We were referred to as the "little guys" by our parents and family, which was ironic because we were always tall for our age.

When we moved in, our house didn't have running water or sewer, so Dad's priority was to drill a well and install a septic system. The well only produced two quarts of water a minute, so on Saturday bath nights, Karen and Brenda got the water first, and then Loren and I took our turn. We also shared rooms, with Loren and I in one, Karen and Brenda in another, and Lowell occupying a wide spot in the hallway he claimed as his own. On hot summer nights, Loren and I would crawl out the window onto the dormer of our bedroom. We'd sit on the roof, talk, and watch the traffic go by until Mom or Dad would catch us and tell us to come inside.

We attended Poplar Grade School for first through eighth grade. It was walking distance from our house, just a quarter mile away. Although there was a bus, we preferred to walk or take our bicycles to school, regardless of the weather. Our town's most famous resident was Richard Ira Bong, the WWII "Ace of Aces," who flew a P-38 Lightning and shot down forty Japanese enemy aircraft in the South Pacific. He is still the pride of Poplar. I grew up with some of Richard's nephews and nieces and am still in touch with them. The elementary school had a trophy room attached to the school with history displayed there. They also exhibited Richard's gleaming, silver P-38 outside our school until they restored it and moved it to its new home at the Richard I. Bong World War II Heritage Center.

In the winter, the lake effect from Lake Superior would heap cold and snow on our little town and school would be canceled. If it were too cold, we would stay inside. Otherwise, we would be sledding or playing with our friends in the knee-deep snow or zipping around the little skating rink in town with our hockey puck and stick, wearing skates too small that squeezed our toes or skates too large that slowed us down.

My dad, Carroll Johnson, and my mom, Phyllis Peterson, spent most of their lives in Poplar. The first Johnson to come to America from Sweden was my dad's grandfather, Andrew Johnson. He was a "fire and brimstone" preacher who was among the twelve men who started the Evangelical Covenant Church and North Park College. Dad's father was Fridolph Johnson, a homesteading dairy farmer who died at age thirty-nine when Dad was only ten years old. My mom's dad was Norwegian as well as Swedish. His name was Clifford Peterson, and he was the postmaster of Poplar. My grandfathers knew each other, and their children, Carroll and Phyllis, were born only twelve days apart. The two men often laughed together about how their children would get married someday.

Carroll and Phyllis did eventually meet and became friends through church functions at the Mission Covenant Church, which was always an important spiritual and social center for our town and our family.

It's been said that early on Carroll predicted Phyllis would be his bride. However, Clifford wanted his daughter to become a missionary. He sent her to Wheaton College in Wheaton, Illinois, but Phyllis was instead called to marry Carroll Johnson after only a semester there. They wed in 1947, and although she was raised with some luxuries of the day, she was content with a small farmhouse.

We could always sense the distance between Mom and Grandpa Peterson. We could feel that he thought his daughter could have done better than marry Dad.

*****

Our home was a happy one. My dad was humble, soft-spoken, and very dedicated to my mom and his family. He was half Swede, a quarter Dane, and a quarter Norwegian. His work ethic was one of his most prominent qualities; hard work ran in his veins! We were like the second family he raised because after his dad died, ten-year-old Carroll became the man of the house and helped raise his four younger siblings. He was a compassionate father but not much of a hugger, even though he had a great laugh and sense of humor. He showed his love by teaching his children solid values and as an excellent Boy Scout leader for his sons. He wasn't one to be sarcastic or demean anyone. We all respected him and wanted to please him. If we disappointed him, the look in his eyes would immediately unsettle us. Dad was also a good mentor and teacher, and he wanted us to know how to work with our hands.

Dad understood the value of a dollar, as well as generosity. His family was extremely poor, but his mom made sure they attended church. One Sunday, Dad found a nickel in the pocket of his blue jeans. As he looked around and saw the offering plate coming his way, he struggled with the decision to donate or keep the nickel, but decided it was the right thing to give it to the church. Returning home after church, he reached into his pocket and pulled out another nickel. It brought him to tears as he told us the ending of the story. Dad took it as a miracle to demonstrate that God would always provide.

Like my father, my mother, Phyllis, lost a parent when she was young. Her mom, Mabel, died when she was four. Grandpa Peterson married Florence three years later. They had a son, Paul (Pep) Peterson, who was seven years younger than Phyllis.

Once married and happily settled as a wife and mother, Mom carried out her own mission. Her life was busy and full between caring for her family and friends in the community. She was very involved with her children, in Boy and Girl Scouts, and just keeping the home fires burning. She was Dad's right hand and bookkeeper. She was often seen in the kitchen in her apron, from where she could easily watch her children playing in the yard or shooting basketballs into the hoop on the front of our garage.

Mom was soft-spoken and direct, and known for her famous sweet rolls, which she always seemed to have on hand for her hungry family or unexpected visitors. From her six-seat table in the kitchen, she held court, receiving friends who would drop in to seek her advice on topics ranging from childrearing to Christian living. After I was on my own, I heard that mom's friends continued to stop in and get the benefit of her experience on how to deal with "these kids!" Perhaps raising me gave her wisdom beyond anyone else's years!

*****

I grew up in a busy home. Dad was often improving the house or garage area with my Grandpa Peterson and Mom's Uncle Irvin while he ran his logging business out of the property. He needed a growing storage space for the tools and vehicles of his business. Meanwhile, his employees would come and go, picking up their paychecks.

Dad was an independent, self-proprietor in the pulpwood logging business. He bought his equipment and upgraded it himself when he could see a better and more productive approach to increasing production. The aspen trees he felled supplied pulpwood to Superwood in Duluth, Minnesota and Superior Fiber Products in Superior. They both produced hardboard used in car and truck door panels and particle board panels from wood pulp.

During the spring, while the sap was running in the aspen trees, he hired crews to hand peel the bark to ship to the paper mills in Wisconsin. The days of hand peeling bark ended with the invention of the automated log debarker. However, Dad would tell us about his best year, when he shipped sixty railroad cars full of peeled wood.
Pulpwood logging was strenuous, dangerous work with limited income and rewards. When Dad bought a shear, it eliminated the

most dangerous part of the operation. The machine was a powerful, four-wheel drive tractor with a large, hydraulic-powered blade that sliced through the tree and guided the direction the tree fell. Dad was also the first logger in the area to employ pole skidders, machines to manipulate full-length trees. Since his trucks only accommodated logs and pulpwood eight feet in length, he bought a "slasher," which would cut the complete logs to fit them onto the truck and load them for delivery to the mill. Such handling was new to the local area, but others didn't take long to follow his lead. Dad also added axles to his trucks to haul larger payloads in compliance with the weight restrictions of trucks on the highways. Some laughed at his ideas, but the producers soon added axles to their trucks. Dad hired men for many years until he could buy equipment to automate more work. Eventually, he could produce a truckload of logs per day by himself.

Dad logged most of the wood (stumpage) on county land put up for bid. He sometimes logged on an inexpensive tract near Lake Superior, which was allowed only in winter when the ground was frozen. Stumpage was cheaper there, but it was still a challenging way to make a living. The cost of supplying wood to the plants was high, and the mills showed no loyalty to the full-time loggers. Construction workers would go logging when their jobs ended in summer and glut the market until Christmastime. The cost of operating the equipment, insurance, and fuel left very little extra at the end of the month. I remember mom declaring, "We are insurance poor," or "We have to rob Peter to pay Paul," as she and my dad worked hard to "stretch the dollars." Equipment payments and payroll always took precedence over dad's salary.

Dad worked a six-day workweek and took Sunday to rest. He never missed church and was an active volunteer there. On his one day of rest, my siblings and I would beg him to take us swimming, to see our cousins, or help us with other activities. We knew he was tired, but he would always rise to the occasion. I always respected Dad and the work he did, and I also liked the fact he drove trucks and equipment. We weren't rich, but neither were many other families in the area. We never missed a meal and always had nice clothes to wear. Dad would even take time off from work to take a vacation each year, and when we were in Boy Scouts, he went on canoe trips and other fun scout outings with us.

Much of the time, Dad worked alone in the woods, but he never complained. During the weekdays, he was gone from seven o'clock in the morning until after dark. There were many family dinners without Dad. As we awaited his return, Mom would watch the clock nervously.

"If your dad isn't home by nine o'clock, we will go looking for him," she would say. Then he usually pulled into the yard with his loaded truck and sat down for dinner.

We would all breathe a sigh of relief, knowing that accidents happened in logging all the time and could be serious, especially with nobody around to help. Even so, Loren and I started working in the pulpwood logging business at a very young age.

"Take the little guys with you today," Mom would say to Dad, and off we went.

I'm not sure if Dad needed help or Mom just wanted a break from her two mischievous young boys. We were expected to be productive "in the woods," and we were happy to be spending time with Dad.

One day, when I was twelve and Loren was fourteen, Dad was on his little John Deere 350 bulldozer loading 100-inch pulpwood with his hydraulic skid loader. Loren and I were on the ground next to the dozer when Loren accidentally stepped between the dozer and skid loader. Dad didn't see him and reversed the dozer, pinning Loren's leg to the ground. With a horrifying scream from Loren, Dad pulled ahead and released Loren's leg.

We knew Loren's leg was seriously broken, and we had to get him to the hospital ASAP. We had traveled to our worksite in our pulp-hauling truck so it would have to be our "ambulance." Carefully, Dad and I lifted Loren into the truck, and I laid his broken leg on my lap for the trip to the medical care he needed in Superior. It was the longest forty miles I ever traveled, and the rough-riding truck was not a comfortable vehicle to transport an injured person. Poor Loren winced with pain the whole time.

"Hold on, Loren," I told him helplessly. "Dad is driving as fast as he can."

The doctors told us the break was very serious in someone so young and as Loren continued to grow, he may develop a short leg.

Fortunately, Loren's leg fully recovered, grew normally, and he did not even develop a limp. However, none of us ever forgot how vigilant you must be around heavy equipment and how one small mistake can have life-long consequences.

*****

Loren and I had many adventures at the family home. We spent hours in the sandbox together. At Christmas, we were given quality steel Tonka trucks and dirt-moving toys. In the spring, Dad had a five cubic-yard dump truck deliver a load of sand in a low area next to the garage. By fall, Loren and I had the five yards leveled out using only our toy trucks and equipment. This went on for several years until the low area was at grade, and we were on to other activities like peeling trees with Dad's crew, mowing the lawn, and operating actual logging equipment.

Growing up, Loren and I shared toys and played Little League, but Loren lost interest in sports while young. I shot hoops in front of the garage while Loren was inside, taking something apart just to see how it was built or adjusting it so it operated better. This is where we differed the most and the place Loren seemed happiest. He loved to disassemble and reassemble objects to improve their function. This love, discovered in his youth, continued into adulthood.

Together, we were a handful for my mother. She used to say, "What one doesn't think of, the other one does!" For example, Loren and I built a very crude go-kart. Loren had the idea of taking the 18-horsepower engine out of his snowmobile and mounting it onto the go-kart. It was also difficult to mount a muffler onto the cart, so we attached a megaphone in place of the muffler. You can only imagine how loud it was! We raced it around the circle drive of our house, spitting rocks and raising dust for hours.

One afternoon, Loren ventured onto US Highway 2 and headed into the village of Poplar. I stood in the driveway, watching and waiting for Loren to return. Mom saw me and came outside.

"Brian where is Loren?" she asked.

At that exact moment, Loren and the go-kart screamed past the house on Highway 2 at top speed. Mom just stood there with her mouth agape.

That wasn't the first or last time our go-kart ventured off the property and into the village of Poplar. We were always exploring new places to ride. There was another family of boys in Poplar with a go-kart, and the rumor was they were sometimes blamed for our escapades.

Another time Loren and I were fishing under a bridge about a mile from our home. We were getting a little bored, so when I heard a car coming, I cast my line up to the highway with a bait fish on my hook. Somehow the fish attached itself to a car. I stood holding my fish pole as my line snapped and my reel and line trailed out of sight behind my catch. My fishing afternoon was over, and we laughed, wondering what the driver would think when he got to his destination and saw a fish attached to his car.

When Loren and I were just ten years old, Dad would start the welder in the garage and set us up with a piece of steel and a welding stinger for us to practice welding. By the age of sixteen, I was driving his truck delivering loads to the mills. Of course, this was before the government required a Commercial Driver's License (CDL) to drive heavy trucks.

* * * * *

When I was thirteen and Loren was fifteen, Dad decided it would be a good idea to excavate the basement. Our house was on a hillside, and by digging the dirt away from the house on the downhill side, Dad wanted to expand the small existing basement and create a walkout. He removed the dirt and Dad set up eight-foot jacks to support the side of the house. Then he took us downstairs to explain our part of the project.

In front of us was a wall of hard red clay, a pick, two shovels, and a wheelbarrow. We were shorter than the dirt wall, so all we could see was clay. The first day of any big project is daunting, but we dug in. We picked and shoveled all day and hardly made a dent in what would be our fall and winter project.

Slowly but surely, Loren and I dug our way around the perimeter of the new basement area, wheeling the red clay outside and away from the house. Next, we dug a trench for a concrete footing to support the new cinder block wall. We hand-mixed the "mud" and carried the twelve-inch blocks to Grandpa Peterson, who built the walls. Seeing the walls emerge around us gave us a sense of our accomplishment. We could even envision the new large room under our house and its value to the home. With the walls completed, it was time to remove the huge pile of clay in the center of what would be our new basement. Loren and I both knew Dad was working too hard to help, except for some time on Saturday, setting up additional supports for the house. It was up to us!

At first, the task again seemed daunting but became easier when we began to see progress. The pile of dirt in the center of the new room disappeared a little more each day. Loren and I spent every spare moment working on our dirt-moving project. We would come home from school, do our homework, maybe attend a Scout meeting or work on activities, and then head downstairs. It was an exciting time, and Loren and I felt a sense of pride that we had accomplished such an incredible task ourselves. Two young kids that were not afraid of hard work! This set the stage for a career of setting goals and being successful.

When the pile of dirt was finally gone, we started grading for the new concrete floor. We were preparing for the day when a crew would pour the concrete to unite the old and new basements and finally complete the project. I will always remember the first day we were allowed to walk on the new floor in our enormous, new room. I brought my bicycle down and took a victory lap!

Dad compensated us for the dirt removal project and taught us to be productive by paying us piecework rather than by the hour. He promised to pay ten cents for each wheelbarrow of dirt we wheeled out to the fill area, earning Loren and I each a nickel per wheelbarrow. When the project was done, we calculated what Dad owed us. The total came to about $125 each! In his infinite wisdom, Dad suggested we buy a life insurance policy with this windfall of money. We purchased a whole life policy that was paid up at age sixty-five. My one 125-dollar whole life insurance payment was due every October for fifty years. I finally made my last payment in 2019. I laugh when I tell others that my dad helped me keep the first nickel I ever earned! Soon, Loren and I went on to work in the logging business with Dad. I was thirteen and Loren was fifteen. In the first summer we worked, we both made $1,000 and bought our first Arctic Cat snowmobiles. Our close friends all had snowmobiles, and we rode with them several nights a week. These were great times and memories with our friends.

*****

Loren was quiet, humble, and kind. It took a lot to get him angry, and in all our years together, I seldom saw him show his temper. We had the normal difficulties brothers may have getting along, but mostly, we were very close and depended on each other in our early years.

We looked quite a bit alike and were often taken for twins

rather than brothers. We were both tall, with dark hair and in good shape from our lives of physical labor. I was a little taller than Loren, eventually hitting six feet four while he stopped growing at six feet two. I looked more like Dad, with a longer, thinner face. Loren had the rounder, Scandinavian looks of Mom.

Working with Dad gave us our education in time management and sacrifice to become self-employed in the future. I played football in high school, and we started football practice in August. I would work all day in the woods and, on occasion, deliver the load of wood and drive the truck to football practice. The coach would commend me for the dedication to the team, as I was co-captain.

After high school Loren went on to Wisconsin Indianhead Technical College (WITC) which is today known as Northwood Technical College and enrolled in Auto Mechanics classes. After graduation, he was hired to work at Cummins Diesel in Duluth, Minnesota. Loren firmly believed that "if a man could build it, we can fix it." It didn't surprise anyone when he took apart his brand-new Dodge Duster to install new high-performance upgrades. Whenever I had a repair that was giving me difficulty, I depended on Loren and his experience and abilities.

On June 15, 1973, Loren married his high school sweetheart, Delores (Deed) Gustafson, a quieter, more serious girl with blond hair. Delores had just finished her chosen career training in cosmetology. They rented a house in Wentworth, Wisconsin, just a few miles from Poplar.

When I graduated from high school, I was offered two sports scholarships to college—one to play football and the other to play basketball, but I knew I wanted to pursue a career with heavy equipment in construction. I never regretted my choice. I went to work for D.L. Johnson and Sons (no relation!) Construction, driving trucks and operating heavy equipment. I was working in Wisconsin and Minnesota in different locations and would live there, returning to Poplar on the weekends. During the winter months, I left the frigid Wisconsin temperatures and found work in the warmer climates of Texas and California. Loren, Deed, and I spent a lot of time together on weekends with our snowmobiles and building and racing Volkswagen dune buggies in the sand country of Highland and Barnes, Wisconsin. It was just the beginning of our adventures together.

*****

In 1977, when I was twenty-two and Loren was twenty-four, we decided to buy and restore an old hand sawmill. Dad encouraged our purchase, as he had just bought a sizable 24 x 6 lumber planer that could create a finished board from rough-sawn lumber. He also had the equipment to plane tongue-and-groove paneling and tongue-and-groove decking. He hoped to retire from the logging business and use the planer as a retirement income source. Together with Dad's equipment, our mill could saw and plane finished lumber for paneling and decking.

The sawmill had not been active for many years, although I remember Dad taking logs there in the past. The mill was fifteen miles away, but we disassembled it, measured the supports, and moved it behind Dad's house, where we knew we could reassemble it and pour concrete supports. The mill had a forty-eight-inch insert tooth saw and hand carriage and was powered by a gasoline engine and a large flat belt. Since we had access to three-phase power, we rewired it to a 50-horsepower electric motor. We poured concrete pillars as a foundation for the mill and set it up.

Dad found a stumpage sale in Douglas County, and he brought home sixty-thousand board feet of quality Norway and White Pine sawlogs. Loren and I spent every opportunity in the spring of 1977 sawing and dry piling the lumber. I was waiting for my summer construction job to start, and Loren was still working at Cummins Diesel. We would saw until Loren had to leave for work at three o'clock in the afternoon. I would spend the rest of the day dry piling what we sawed that day.

The sawmill changed my life and encouraged me to set new goals, like buying land and building a house. Loren was planning to build a house for him and Deed, and I was planning to build a garage to live in before I planned out my own home. The lumber would be ready for building as soon as we acquired our land and plans to build our structures. Looking back, it was an amazing experience to transform raw trees into the boards we nailed together ourselves to create our homes. We were blessed to have the opportunity, made by our dad, and all he had taught us in preparation for our labor.

In the fall of 1978, I started framing a 26 x 36 garage on my land, but I spent the winter in Fresno, California. When I returned to Poplar in Spring of 1979, I finished the garage and sectioned off a 26 x 14 area to live in. I drilled a well and installed a septic system. I had all the comforts I needed, with a place to park my vehicle inside. I built a small kitchen, bathroom, and sauna in my living area.

Regardless of how big or small the project was, Loren and I worked well together ninety-nine percent of the time. However, our strength and success later in life was because of Dad and the things he taught us. I truly felt that between the three of us, we could be successful at anything!

JOHNSON
TIMBER
MINING

CHAPTER 2

A CALL TO ADVENTURE

It was early November of 1980, and I was working on a road construction job in Grand Marias, Minnesota, with D.L. Johnson and Sons. By that time, Loren had tired of working in "oil and grease," as he called it. He was ready for a change. He quit Cummins Diesel and joined Dad in the logging industry.

One day after work, I received a message to call Loren. When he picked up the phone, he didn't mince words. "Dad's hurt," he said. It was a call I had been dreading. It's a known fact that logging is one of the most dangerous occupations there is. Dad had been hurt before, several times, and had also had some close calls. One summer my sister Brenda was working with him operating his pole skidder. She had backed up six trees and hooked the cables to each one to pull them over to the landing and the slasher. Dad was on the ground behind Brenda, cutting the branches and tops off the trees. Brenda pulled the trees up to the back of the skidder using the attached winch. One of the trees slid under the skidder, and as she pulled on it, the top of the tree lifted and hit Dad on the side of the head. The impact knocked him to the ground out cold. Brenda jumped off the machine and ran to him, but he had already risen to his feet. They checked him out at the hospital, and he was okay. But the injury could easily have been fatal.

Then there was the time Loren and Dad were working together and Loren was on the skidder. Again, dad was cutting the branches and tops off the trees and Loren started to pull the trees toward the landing. One of the trees in tow hooked on a stump and the top of the tree whipped past Dad, caught the fly of his pants, and ripped the front. Truly, a close call!

This time, Loren explained that a similar incident had occurred with the pole skidder and Dad's hip had been struck by one of the logs. Amazingly, the hip did not break but it was severely bruised. Also, since he was recuperating from one injury, Dad had decided to take care of a prostate operation he had been delaying. He would be off his feet for at least two weeks.

"Can you come back to Poplar and help out till he's better?" Loren asked me.

The timing was good because the construction project was almost done. I left that night, and the next day Loren and I were once again working together. We understood the dangers of logging and how quickly one of us could be injured, but we had always accepted work as part of life. Dad was now in his fifties and in a good place. He was content, his equipment was paid off, and he made a comfortable living. Still, after the accident, for the very first time ever, Loren and I began to wonder if it was time for Dad to leave the logging business.

*****

Many of my childhood memories are tied to my dad's sister Lois, her husband, Roger Green, and their family. Uncle Roger was a very kind-hearted man and always had time for his nephews and nieces. He had a big smile, a hearty laugh, and never missed church on Sundays. Roger always had a shack in the woods. First, it was in the woods near Lake Superior on the same land where Dad had logged in the winter months, and later, when he moved to Duluth, he built a shack in Minnesota. He would live there during the week, sawing lumber and returning home on the weekends. Aunt Lois was a typical Scandinavian, big-boned, but not heavy, who easily spoke her mind. They were both wonderful to us.

Loren and I were very close to our cousin, Doug, who was a year older than me and a year younger than Loren. When Loren and I were nine and ten years old, the Greens lived on a farm they named "Green Acres" in Cloverland, which was about ten miles from Poplar. When we visited, we were a gang of "wood rats," combing the forest for animals or whatever adventure we could find.

I wasn't surprised when Doug attended the University of Minnesota in Duluth after graduation. He was a force that made things happen. Later, he attended Utah State University, where he earned a master's degree in geology. Doug was always determined, looking ahead, and planning his next move, which brought him to Alaska. He jumped at the chance to prospect mining claims on Sourdough Creek for claim owners, and made the trip to the 66-mile marker on Steese Highway, northeast of Fairbanks.

Doug was impressed enough by what he saw on Sourdough Creek to ask the owners to let him set up his own mining operation. Together with Roger, Lois, his younger brother Tim and another family, Doug had set out in the summer of 1979 to start their mining adventure in Alaska. They were successful the first year, but the two families amicably decided it would be more lucrative for to work separately on different mining claims. Now, just a few days after Dad's injury, Doug and Roger wanted a meeting with us.

As I sat down with Dad, Loren, Doug, and Roger, I had no idea what we were going to talk about. Mom had the coffee and sweet rolls ready as we filled the six chairs around the kitchen table where so much wisdom had been shared.

Doug told us that he knew of minable claims on Birch Creek, just off the scenic Steese Highway. In short, Doug and Roger suggested we could successfully mine the land for gold given our experience and know-how. Loren and I were completely surprised. We knew Doug and Uncle Roger had been mining gold, but we never thought we could have the opportunity to do the same. We knew they had been somewhat successful, and we felt very comfortable following their lead.

They explained that we could mine near the claim they had worked in the Summer of 1980. We could pattern our operation after theirs, using a dragline, D8 Caterpillar dozer, and sluice box to get started. There was an excited energy in the air, as Dad, Loren, and I eagerly took notes and absorbed everything they explained about the equipment we needed and the process itself. Everybody was excited—except Mom. She was pouring the coffee and shaking her head in disbelief at the conversation. In her mind, it was a far-fetched and crazy plan and secretly hoped Dad would come to his senses before committing to the idea.

Uncle Roger explained the different ways to mine for gold and how we would be "placer" mining. Placer gold mining extracts gold from deposits in rivers, streams, or ancient riverbeds. We were surprised to learn that it was very easy to apply for and receive a permit for a mining operation and that we already had the claim area. We would have to prepare the site by constructing infrastructure to divert flowing water, strip the overburden (organic black muck and non-paying clean upper gravels), and wash the gold bearing gravels with the sluice box.

Doug began making a list of the equipment, tools, and living necessities we would need to get started. We already had much of it already, as well as lumber and plywood for the cabins we would build to live in. The night after the meeting, Dad, Loren, and I met again around the table to continue the discussion between the three of us. We were unanimously onboard. The plan was in motion, and we discussed how to obtain the needed equipment, which included a large crane to work for us as a dragline, an engine for supplying power for a very large water pump, and other smaller pieces of equipment. Not only would we need to buy the equipment, but we would have to transport it to the mining claims.

Life glowed a little brighter as we began making mental plans for a big life change. Dad decided to let his business lay idle for a bit while in Alaska. Deed was willing to leave her job at the beauty shop and join Loren for the adventure.

As for me, I was dating a girl named Suzy at the time. Suzy lived in Superior and had a good job as a data processor for the Wisconsin Department of Transportation. We had been dating for a year and neither one of us was ready for a long-term commitment. Suzy was content to stay in Wisconsin and decided we would be able to stay in touch with phone calls.

The only holdout was Mom. She made no secret of the fact she was praying God would put a roadblock in front of us before it was too late. She didn't understand the timing of the decision. Dad's logging equipment was paid for and in good condition. Why would he go back into debt for a crazy, risky business in Alaska of all places? Yet, plans persisted. We were unstoppable and once Mom realized we were going, she was with us all the way. My parents had a saying in the family: "Peace at any price." Mom got ready to pay the price.

Our master plan was to finish logging and making plans through the winter, and then set off for Alaska in April. Everything we did had an undertone of excitement and purpose as we moved towards our big life change.

*****

In the winter of 1980, I had made plans to spend the winter in Breckenridge, Colorado, working at a ski resort with a couple of friends. I changed my plans on a dime after we made the decision to go to Alaska. I let my friends go without me because I had to help with the preparations. I can honestly say I have never regretted the decision. It was the start of a new, challenging career for me.

1981 arrived with the usual, cold, blustery January Poplar weather. One morning it was five degrees below zero and the wind was howling at thirty miles per hour, Loren and I talked on the phone and decided it was too miserable to work that day. Not long afterwards, we each got a call from Mom.

"I know it's cold, but can you go out today? I have a few bills I need to pay, and I could sure use a check for a load," she asked, sheepishly.

Of course, we put on our cold weather gear and went to work. I could understand the need for us to be producing, even in the miserable weather. The three of us were now drawing an income from the logging operation. We knew it wouldn't be long before we were mining in the Alaskan summer sun. With any luck, we wouldn't have to do any logging the following winter!

*****

As we purchased equipment for our gold mining operation, Mom continued praying that our plans would fall through. Much to her dismay though, everything seemed to easily fall into place.

We found a 1948 Koehring crane in Duluth that had been sitting idle for a time. It was a good-sized machine with a seventy-foot boom, and we purchased it for $13,000. A dragline could move dirt for pennies a yard and it is good for stacking dirt in high places, saving room, and storing large quantities of dirt in small areas. We intended to use it to process pay dirt (hopefully containing gold) through a sluice box and dig drainage. The only repair it needed was the fairlead, which guides the drag cable on the winch that pulls and loads the bucket on the crane. The seller agreed to have a used fairlead installed before the crane left Duluth. He also had a four-thousand-gallon fuel tank to hold the fuel that would keep our engines turning and power our heavy equipment and camp needs. Finally, we also located a dragline bucket that worked well with the crane.

The dragline seller agreed to dismantle the crane and get it to the railyard for the two-month journey to Alaska. We planned to have all our equipment shipped simultaneously to Seattle, where it would continue aboard a barge to Anchorage. From there, the equipment would be hauled by truck the hundred miles north to our claims in Birch Creek.

As the months flew by, the seller procrastinated. By the time he committed to a date to get our equipment to the railyard, it was March, and the city had declared "Spring Breakup." This is a time when heavy loads are not allowed on the roads because the thaw during Spring makes them vulnerable to damage. The dragline was 104,000 pounds, well over the weight limit, but the dragline seller needed to get it to Alaska for its summer work.

In an unusual move by Dad, he appointed Loren and I to go

to Duluth to get the dragline to the railyard. We knew there was no way of reducing the weight of the machine, but working together we could at least use two trucks: one moving the crane itself and the other moving the sections of the boom. It was not lost on us that this was one of the first times Dad stepped back and let us take the lead on solving a seemingly insurmountable problem. We safely moved the crane to the railyard and used plenty of hardwood blocking and cable to secure it for the long trip north. We would see it again when we unloaded it off a semi-truck on Birch Creek.

One by one, we checked off the equipment we needed for the trip. Loren procured an engine from a junk yard in Duluth that had been owned by the US Air Force. We would use it to power the water pump to feed the sluice box. The engine had only been used 250 hours, but after draining the oil, we saw that the Air Force mechanics had not filled it to the necessary oil level. The bearings seized on the crankshaft. Luckily, Loren and I were able to have it running again smoothly in a few days by polishing the crankshaft and installing good, used rod and crankshaft bearings.

We needed a water pump, so Dad had made a trip to Glendive, Montana, and brought back a Crisafulli pump. The high-volume, low-pressure pump designed for irrigation was perfect for our mining operation. We attached a truck transmission to the engine so we could have variable speed as we fed water to our sluicing system. We also bought pre-shaped steel to build the sluice box.

For shelter, we needed to build cabins on our claims. Dad had a pallet of plywood in stock for that purpose. We scavenged for household items like heaters, refrigerators, and other items and found beds, dressers, and smaller water pumps and generators to furnish our cabins and the camp. I donated a water heater from my house that I had fashioned from a sixteen-gallon beer keg to heat my sauna water. We found an old-fashioned Maytag wringer washer for our laundry, and tools of all kinds to assemble, build, repair, and tweak anything in the mining operation.

As the news of our plan to head north and mine gold traveled like wildfire through our small town, people approached us to help with our big move. A fellow who was planning to drive his semi-trailer truck to Alaska to transport freight to Prudhoe Bay from Fairbanks and Anchorage offered to help us move our equipment. He had a forty-foot refrigerated trailer, outfitted to haul freight that had been upgraded to handle the extreme weather conditions of Alaska. This agreement was a win-win, as we desperately needed to transport supplies, and we would cover the cost of his trip.

The trucker was warned that hauling our supplies would damage the interior of his refrigerated trailer. However, we took great care to protect the walls as we filled the trailer with steel, lumber, appliances, engines, pumps, and other freight. When the doors were closed for the final time, the trailer was loaded to the maximum with our Alaskan supplies, nearly two feet from the ceiling and all the way back to the doors. We agreed to pay him forty-five hundred for the trip and told him we'd meet him in Birch Creek.

Our good friend, Conrad Johnson, had an old, but sturdy 1970 Dodge utility truck we lovingly named "Big Red." It had been owned by a telephone company and was the perfect size and set up for hauling fuel, a welder, cutting torches, and tools. A long-time friend from Poplar, Mitch Erickson, who I had worked side by side with the D. L. Johnson and Sons, expressed interest in working with us and riding with me. Another friend from Poplar, Brad Olson, was traveling to Anchorage and decided to travel with us in his own car with another high school friend, Calvin Pearson. Calvin wanted to make the trip to Alaska to help us get started. He was a carpenter and would be a big help building the camp cabins. Brad would ride with us until the Tok cutoff, which is the principal access route to Anchorage from the Alaskan Highway.

Our plans were made, and everything was assembled. Now we were ready for the big move. And we expected that would be an adventure in itself!

CHAPTER 3

ADVENTURE BEGINS

On a sunny day in April, Mitch, Calvin, Brad, and I set out on the 3,400-mile, five-day drive from Poplar to Birch Creek in the scant comfort of Big Red. To ease our journey, Scott Lundberg recorded some great music for us, and I installed a good Alpine cassette player. It was a rough-riding, uncomfortable vehicle for our trip, but the great music made it bearable.

Our route was set. From Poplar we headed west to Duluth, then on to Grand Forks, North Dakota. From Grand Forks we drove straight north to Winnipeg, then west to Saskatoon, Saskatchewan. Just before pulling into the town for the night, the music that had distracted and entertained us for so long mysteriously quit. The Alpine player had played its last tape!

I couldn't imagine the rest of the miles without music. I headed straight to the electronics store to replace the player, but the purchase would cost me $600, which was not in the budget! I left the store saddened that we would have to continue without music.

It took Mitch and me a few miles to get used to the silence, but we continued onto Edmonton, then to Dawson Creek, British Columbia, where we would arrive at mile one, Alaska Highway. Once there, we were finally out of the prairies and our desire for music was replaced by a satisfaction with the changing scenery. Everywhere we looked we saw verdant hills, beautiful deciduous forests, and picturesque valleys.

As there was no GPS in those days, we had purchased a "Mile

Post" book to help us navigate the Alaska Highway. It was imperative for planning the journey because it pointed out the mile markers for gasoline, accommodations, and restaurants which were few and far between along the lonely, rural route. The Alaska Highway would take us through Fort St. John and Fort Nelson in British Columbia, then through Watson Lake and Whitehorse in the Yukon Territory.

One of the highlights of the trip was passing through Haines Junction, and the sight of the beautiful Kluane National Park, with its white-capped, rough-hewn mountains, rising majestically before us. We crossed the border into Alaska at Beaver Creek. At Tok, we said goodbye to Brad, who continued to travel southeast to Anchorage, while we continued northwest to Fairbanks.

Other than the loss of our music, the trip was uneventful for us. We were thankful to arrive in Fairbanks for a fuel stop. Then we made our way up the beautiful, scenic passageway through the Alaskan wilderness known as the Steese Highway. The Steese is also known as Alaska Route 6 and extends from Fairbanks to Circle, a community on the Yukon River. When you hit Birch Creek, you are only fifty miles from the Arctic Circle.

Today, in addition to the scenic forests, and Black Spruce-dotted rolling hills, you see the occasional hiking trail or parking lot under the protection of the Alaskan Bureau of Land Management. You can even see working mines or abandoned gold dredges, bridges, and a glimpse of the Alaskan pipeline around mile eight of the highway.

Our claims stood on mile one hundred of the Steese Highway, between Twelve Mile Summit and Eagle Summit, two snow-capped mountains around three thousand feet in elevation. We were yet to discover that these two mountains would influence our summer weather, often bringing cold, wind, and rain to our camp. As we arrived, though, we rejoiced in reaching our destination safely, and greeted Mom and Dad, who were already on the property with their thirty-foot, fifth-wheel RV. Mom had always liked camping, so she was already feeling at home in the new environment. She especially liked that we were right off the highway.

"I'm so glad we can see people!" she exclaimed happily, as she had been dreading isolation at camp.

As time went on, Mom was also happily connected to the rest of the world through the radio show, "Trapline Chatter." The show was broadcast from the powerful, 50,000-Watt AM radio station KJNP located in North Pole, Alaska. Friends and relatives could call messages into the station which they would read on the show for one-way communication to people who lived in remote bush areas of the great northwest. Every evening, Mom religiously listened to Trapline Chatter for messages from family and friends.

One of her grandkids was born during the summer months in Alaska, and we used Trapline Chatter to receive the news. The first year at camp, Mom came with her plane ticket in hand to get back to my sister, Brenda, in time to help with her first baby. She had to guess a date for the return flight and the travel agent got it right. Mom was landing in Minneapolis-St. Paul just as my niece, Sheri, born. She sent us the message of Sheri's birth on Trapl .. As the years went by, we received many other greetings ıds and family planning to visit us at the mine.

The semi-truck with our gear had arrived before Calvin, and I arrived at the creek. Loren and Dad had unloa and our equipment and supplies were strewn in a clearing, rea aim. The driver was pleased that our careful packing had protected the inside of his trailer. However, he did request an additional thousand dollars over the agreed amount because of several unexpected costs during his trip, including lengthy detours and weather delays.

The first order of business was to begin work on the cabins for our camp. The plan was to have one for me and Mitch and one for Deed and Loren. Until that time, Mitch and I were staying in an old trapper's cabin and Loren and Deed stayed in the RV with Mom and Dad.

We set about constructing the barebones, four-walled, plywood structures with a roof, a door, and two windows. Construction took about a week to complete. Mitch and I shared one big room that measured 12 x 18 feet with a bed each and a box for our clothes. A small portion in the back of our cabin was used for indoor camp storage. Deed made a simple sign that read, "Johnson's Mining Co." and posted it outside the cabin.

Loren and Deed had luxury quarters, including a small kitchenette and a table and chairs to eat dinner. Deed insisted that she and Loren have dinner together alone every evening. Deed and Loren only joined us to celebrate special occasions, but Mitch and I ate with Mom and Dad every night. The couple also had an indoor bathroom which used an RV toilet that Loren hooked up to a water source, along with a shower. We built a camp outhouse, and Mitch and I showered in the RV.

As we concerned ourselves with the operation of the mine, Mom and Deed set their domestic routine. The biggest thorn in their side was laundry day. Laundry day was once a week and a stressful time for them both. It was an inconvenient task because all we had was the old Maytag wringer washer. The only dryer we had was a few strung clotheslines in the rough wooded area behind our camp. And as you can imagine, our laundry was filled with unusually soiled garments.

Deed insisted her clothes be washed first in the clean water and the rest added later. The Johnson credo was "peace at any price," and this was the first indication that Deed wasn't planning to play by all the rules. Deed couldn't understand why we needed to work so many days a week and long into the evening. She had grown up in a union home with set work hours, and we had been self-employed most of our lives. We had also borrowed money to start this venture, and the season to recoup it was about one hundred days. The rest of us were on a mission to succeed in a short period of time.

Despite her shortcomings, Deed was a good cook and a cleaning fanatic when it came to her home and kitchen. Deed liked it when things were organized well. She was meticulous in everything she did.

When we finished the cabins, we were still awaiting delivery on the dragline and other equipment we had shipped from Poplar, as well as a Cat D8 bulldozer which we had leased from a dealer in Fairbanks. It was a 1974 model with new tracks and front idlers and seemed ready for work. It was the most expensive piece of equipment we had, but it was also the heart of the operation and a great match for the dragline.

We knew Alaska had road restriction weight limits in place. We had to patiently wait until the restrictions were lifted, which happened on June 1. The delay in getting our equipment didn't slow us down; we had plenty to do. First, we had to fabricate a sluice box, which is a channeled chute-like apparatus to receive dirt, sand, and sediment. We fashioned it from eight-foot lengths of steel we had transported from Poplar, creating channels by welding them together. With the help of a running water source, the sluice box carries a slurry through the channel over "riffles" in the bottom of the sluice that creates a vortex to trap the heavier materials. Since gold is nineteen times heavier than water and the black sand of Birch Creek was eight times heavier, the riffles capture the gold and the black sand. Lighter materials are discharged and called "tailings." We set our sluice box at one and seven-eighths inch per foot slope to create the highest possible recovery rate for the gold.

We then built a steel "head box" which is the area that receives the dirt before it is washed through the twenty-four-foot sluice. We would have to closely monitor the water flow to maximize material processing without overloading it so the gold would not be carried over the box with the lighter brown sand and other tailings. We would sluice the concentrated materials through a smaller apparatus to be sure no gold was lost. Nuggets were non-existent along the banks of Birch Creek. We were hunting for fine gold flakes and specks, and it is a known fact you can never stop all the gold with a conventional sluice box.

A week later, the sluice was finished, and we set the whole mining operation structure on skids so it could easily be moved to the next location once an area had been mined out. We patterned our mining setup after Doug's, although we knew we would be making changes to maximize gold recovery. No two mining operations are the same, and we could tell that a great deal of our mining time would be spent tweaking the riffles and other parts of our mining operation. Soon after, our dirt-moving equipment was delivered, and it was time to start mining!

*****

We had signed a lease for five separate claims on Birch Creek from a fellow in Fairbanks and agreed to pay the lease holder ten percent of the gold we recovered. Doug's family was mining on the creek nearby, about a mile north. We found out there were other miners in this gold-rich area and knew of two operations on Eagle Creek and three on nearby Gold Dust Creek.

We began panning our claim to find the perfect spot to set up the mining operation. The notion of "panning" sounds primitive and often conjures up images of desperate, fool-hearty bearded forty-niners in the 1800s. However, serious modern miners still regard it as the best way to determine the location for a mining operation. Being the greenhorns we were, Cousin Tim had to show us how to pan correctly. Doug's brother Tim matched me in height but now bent his wiry frame over to scoop up the sediment material into his pan.

"This is where you want to spend your time prospecting," Tim said, carefully scraping bits of bedrock into his pan.

He explained that through the years, gold settles down through the gravel into the creek bed, where the richest accumulation can be found. He then filled the pan with water to wash the lighter material out and suddenly, something caught my eye. Sure enough! Gleaming in the sun were several pieces of gold—my first sight on our claim. *So, this is what it's all about*, I thought. There *was* gold in these hills! A few more pans confirmed it. We had found our location to set up the sluice box!

The ground had some black spruce trees we needed to push off to the side with the D8 Caterpillar to begin stripping the overburden off the land. Overburden is what we call the excess dirt on top of the pay layer and is the dirt that has been tested to yield little or no gold. Next, we made our first cut, which was the area we sectioned off to mine first. It was 150 x 150 feet with approximately six feet of overburden to move. After a few days' work, we were into the pay dirt, which we knew contained gold. We set the box in place, positioning the pump in the creek, and plumbing the hose to the sluice box. We set up our operation about two hundred feet from the creek, and our permit gave us permission to divert the creek if desired.

It is always a challenge to set up a new mining operation because so much of the work is trial and error. We made many adjustments to the set-up and the cut before we felt even slightly ready to start catching gold. We built a ramp to the head-box to push the pay that would be washed into the sluice box.

Our hopes were high when we began sluicing the first cut. Gold was selling then at about $375 an ounce, and it was our hope to recover at least an ounce an hour. We planned to work twelve-hour days. Every time we shut down the operation, we would check the sluice box for a glimpse of gold. Sure enough, we were seeing gold, but clueless as to the amount and weight. It lay among the riffles, shining in the summer sun. Yes! We were gold miners. At that time, finding any amount of yellow metal in the riffles, no matter how small, was exciting. Checking the sluice box could make our day or depress us depending on what we found. We felt we had a lot to learn about how to mine faster and better, but we were in Alaska, mining gold!

After several days and ongoing tweaks and adjustments, it was time to do what miners call a cleanup. The cleanup is the process of washing the rugs under the riffles that catch and trap the gold. It was hard, back-breaking work to carry and wash the heavy, dirt-laden rugs. We used fifty-gallon steel barrels with water that we cut down specifically for the job. With one of us on each side of them, we rolled the rugs to free the concentrate into the barrels.

We would sluice the concentrate through a long tom, which was a mini-sluice with riffles to catch the finest gold. We would typically recover a little more gold from the larger volume of gravel and black sand, which was common in the creek. Separating the sand from the gold was no easy feat, and one of the many unexpected challenges we faced in the next few weeks, months, and years. We did the best we could with this cleanup until we had what we thought was a sellable product.

We had several cleanups before the first cut was finished, and we bottled up the cleaned gold to make the trip to the gold buyer in Fairbanks. We hoped to earn enough to pay our fuel bill and buy groceries and other supplies in Fairbanks. Since we didn't have a scale, Doug weighed it for us. Much to our surprise and dismay, we had only been producing half an ounce an hour and were going backwards fast. We were consuming about two-hundred fifty gallons of fuel a day and our fuel bill thus far was about $5,000. Our first cut had only produced about five thousand in gold. There were long sad faces in our camp as we wondered where we were headed and what our future looked like as miners.

*****

Under the advice of Doug, we decided to move upstream a few hundred feet to find richer ground. We made another cut and resumed mining. We once again saw that familiar yellow gleam in the water, but now the sight had lost its appeal. We now knew that what we were seeing in the sluice boxes wasn't nearly enough to cover our expenses.

We were working as hard as we could, seven days a week, starting out daily around eight o'clock in the morning and finishing around ten o'clock at night. We only stopped for meals. Six weeks out of the summer, Alaska had sunlight twenty-four hours a day. I remember times when I would be so invigorated by the late-night sunshine, I just kept working. My co-workers soon noticed I wasn't as productive or useful the next day, so I had to force myself to keep standard working hours and go to sleep without the cover of darkness. One particularly discouraging day when we were wondering if our operation would ever pay off, I looked up and saw a strange sight. A man was walking our way, across our land. We immediately figured it was the occupant of the cabin we had seen across the road when we began mining our first cut. As he approached, we could see he was a gruff-looking character in his fifties. We greeted him politely as he reached us.

"You know, you're mining on my land," he said plainly.

It was unbelievable but proved to be true. After reexamining our claim lines, we found that one of the stakes we had used to show the boundary of our leased land was misplaced on a diagonal across his property line. In exchange, the man offered to sell his claim to us for $20,000 or we could pay him $5,000 for the gold we had taken off his claim.

Sadly, he probably knew the state of the claim from the start. He probably even saw us mining the land but waited until we had yielded something to tell us about our accidental infraction. Certainly, he had seen our equipment and operation from his cabin, just as we could see him. We know he had offered us his deal in a mad attempt to get something for land that was bound to pay out very little. In the end, we ended up paying him the five thousand. It was a hard lesson and a mistake we would never make again.

With the unfortunate affair behind us, we continued to move upstream, trying different parts of our claim in hopes of finding better pay dirt. We were continually disappointed, with yields like the first cut. By August we reached the fifth claim at the furthest point up the river and diverted the creek around the cut to start sluicing. The day still proved disappointing as we shut down the operation for the night and headed back to camp.

I was awakened by the sound of thunder that night, but the entire summer had been rainy, so this was nothing new. However, after breakfast we went up to the cut and found that during the night the creek had broken through the berm we had built as a retaining wall. The entire cut was full of water to the rear sprockets of the Cat.

Luckily, Dad had left the D8 on the ramp leading up to the head box. We stared in wonder and gratitude, recognizing how close we came to disaster. The Cat was leased and had it been submerged, the cost of recovery would have bankrupted us.

Even with one disaster averted, we were still in serious trouble financially. Our checking account was very low, and we were selling the little gold we mined to cover our operating expenses. Our earnings were quickly depleted by the cost of fuel, groceries, and supplies. Even driving the hundred miles to the gold dealer in Fairbanks required resources. We were desperate to find richer ground.

It was a difficult time to receive a letter from Suzy, saying she wanted to come to the mine and spend a week with me. Any happiness I had at her impending visit was overshadowed by our mining difficulties. It couldn't have been a worse time to come. Between the long faces in camp and all of us working harder than ever, I couldn't spare much time to spend with her. However, as I drove her back to Fairbanks when she was leaving, I could see that she wasn't as discouraged as I was. She had a stable job to return to and we would see each other when the mining season was over.

Luckily, the mining community is a small world. We knew a gentleman named Richard McCallum who had some claims on Gold Dust Creek that had yet to be mined. We began to consider him our only hope.

Coincidentally, the Greens were also running out of mineable ground on their claims and struggling financially. Together, we approached Richard and were both granted a cut on his lower claim to finish the year with the stipulation that we paid him ten percent of what we mined. With a sigh of relief, we made the deal, hoping it would save our season and the future we dreamed about. In fact, we needed to find enough gold on our new cut to pay our current bills and either continue the lease on the D8, return it to the dealer, or set up a purchase. The fate of our future hung on the next two weeks and how much gold we could find in the cut.

*****

After a day of moving the equipment and setting it up at the new location, we rose to the Alaskan sun and our first day of mining the new cut. Miners need a positive attitude as they start their day, but ours was clouded with tension. This time, we didn't just hope we would find gold… we HAD to find gold.

We started sluicing the cut and gratefully saw the familiar gold specks in the water. But wait—there seemed to be more gold than usual. Larger shards. More of them. Then, we saw more gold in the sluice than we had ever seen before! We smiled at each other and with cautious excitement, worked on. We had done it. We had finally found a place to mine that would pay off!

By now it was late in the season. It was September and the snow was starting to fall. As we poured our last days of labor into our new cut, we could tell the engine on the dragline was in trouble.

It sputtered and whined as it worked its best for us. We had worked it hard all summer, and it was now vocally resigning. Then we saw smoke wafting into the air and a few sparks from the exhaust. The old girl had given us her all for the season. *Just a little longer*, I silently begged her. However, we closed out our last day, knowing there would be no more gold found until next year.

We cleaned the last of the gold out of the sluice box, pulled the engine out of the dragline, and loaded it into the utility truck. The engine would come home with us for the winter, and we would decide its fate. We winterized the camp and made the final trip to Fairbanks. All we needed was two hundred ounces of gold to cover our expenses and purchase the D8. And, thanks to the rich, producing claim of Richard McCallum, we had it!

We visited NC Machinery and finalized papers to purchase the D8 Cat bulldozer that had served us well all summer. At the time, interest rates were high, and they offered us an atrocious rate of nineteen percent on a five-year loan. Unfortunately, we had no option but to take it.

As we bid Alaska goodbye and headed home to Wisconsin, we considered the ups and downs of our adventure. Although we did not have the success we had hoped for, we had learned a lot and knew we could return to Alaska and be successful if we continued finding claims with high concentrations of gold. But would we or not?

CHAPTER 4

TREASURE & TRIALS

Since 1981 had been a marginal year for our mining operation, we had to spend the fall and winter working Dad's logging business. We were also worried about the next mining season. Since the dragline engine had failed and ended our season prematurely, we still had about eight hours of sluicing left on Dick McCallum's cut. However, we needed to repair and reinstall the engine into the dragline to finish up the pay dirt. We also needed to locate additional mining claims if we were going to continue mining for the entire 1982 season.

A few months after returning home, I received a surprising phone call. It was Bernie Karl, one of the very colorful characters we had met in the mining community in Circle Mining District. He had been extremely friendly and a great help to us as we struggled through our first summer of mining. Bernie explained that he had purchased a 1968 bus to transport some of the family heirlooms from his wife, Connie, to Alaska. Bernie wanted me to pick up the bus in Peoria and drive it to Fairbanks, Alaska, that winter. He also told me he would help me find work in Fairbanks before the mining season. I was ready for the adventure and quickly agreed to fly to Peoria.

It was my first flight in a commercial aircraft and the beginning of an adventure I will never forget. I met Bernie's gracious family in Peoria and spent time visiting with them. Then, armed with a credit card for gas and mechanical expenses on the trip, I started home to Poplar to pick up Mitch, who agreed to join me on the adventure.

I zoomed along the Illinois tollway in the big bus, having had experience driving trucks since I was sixteen. The bus was now laden with treasures from Connie's family, closed off from our view in the back. As I paid the tolls along the way, I must have placed my wallet on a flat shelf next to the driver's window. When I reached out to throw my money into the collection basket at one of the stops, I must have accidentally knocked my wallet into it with my elbow. I did not realize what had happened until I was miles down the tollway. When I got home, my wallet arrived in the mail, intact, with all the money and credit cards in place, along with a note from a stranger! What a lucky start to my big trip and a testament to how honest people can be!

After a few weeks back home, I was ready to begin the trip to Fairbanks. I had picked up three friends who wanted to share the experience: Mitch, who had worked with us in our first mining season; Matt Long, who grew up in Poplar with us; and his friend, Lester Korhonen.

On our cold departure day in January 1982, the bus wouldn't start. I called Mom to come over with a vehicle and give my battery a boost.

"Are you sure you want to make this trip?" she asked dubiously, furrowing her brow at the suspect machinery.

Being young and adventurous, I never thought traveling the winter roads of Alaska in an old bus could be dangerous, yet we faced increasing obstacles as we set off. The first challenge was keeping the windshield clear of frost so we could see where we were going.

We were transporting a twenty-pound propane tank, so we attached a space heater to the top and sat it atop a milk crate. Occasionally, the whole thing would tumble down the steps of the bus door and threaten to roll out the bus door.

Our first real mechanical problem happened in Regina, Saskatchewan, when the starter again failed to turn over the engine. Fortunately, we were in the city with access to auto parts. We acquired and installed a rebuilt starter, and we were on our way again.

As we rumbled onto the Alaskan Highway, the temperature seemed to drop with every mile. With our propane heater pointed forward to keep the windshield clear, frost obstructed views out of both sides of the vehicle. The bus failed to warm up to a comfortable temperature throughout the entire trip.

We came to a slow stop as we saw roadblocks up ahead, just before crossing a bridge over the Yukon River. A truck carrying a high load had hit the upper structure of the bridge and did enough damage to force the Yukon Highway Department to close the bridge until they made repairs. Fortunately for us, there was a detour option. They directed us south to Carcross and then north again to Johnsons Crossing on the Alaskan Highway. The detour took a few hours but drove us through beautiful country.

Emerald Lake, rimmed like the Caribbean with a beautiful aqua band in summer, was tranquil and just as brilliant now frozen over and attended by frosty mountains and trees. We continued to Whitehorse and up to Haines Junction for a well-deserved hotel room and sleep. Before we called it a day, and with just one more day on the road before we arrived in Fairbanks, we spent a little time in the bar and enjoyed a few Canadian beers. From that day forward, I have preferred the strong beer from our Canadian neighbors over any American brands.

The next morning, we started north again through Kluane Park, which we appreciated so much on our first trip up. It was equally magnificent viewed in winter, regaled in its snowy best. Soon after, we faced our next challenge—a broken radiator hose. We needed to repair and shorten the hose and refill the antifreeze which Bernie gave us in anticipation of such an event. The only catch was that it was fifty degrees below zero outside. It had not occurred to us what a dangerous situation we faced, stranded on the roadside in such conditions. We could freeze to death if we could not make the repair. But one of us had to try.

After a conversation among us, Lester, who was perhaps the most reckless of the group, said he would do it. He crawled into the engine to make the repair as quickly as possible. As he worked, Lester made several trips in and out of the bus to warm his hands with the propane space heater, which turned out to be a real "lifesaver" in many ways! On one occasion, after a short break, Lester got out of the bus, took off his jacket and shirt and exposed his bare skin to fifty degrees below zero. I'm not exactly sure why he did it other than to brag about it. It surely was not on the "bucket list" for the rest of us on the nut bus! Miraculously, he completed the repair with his digits intact, and we continued our journey.

We were so relieved to reach Fairbanks. We just needed a place to stay. We were offered lodging outside of Fairbanks at a cabin owned by Steve Porten, another miner we met during the summer of 1981 who was working out of town. Lester flew home, Matt found work in Fairbanks, and eventually his wife Dawn joined him, also finding work. Bernie found Mitch and me a job at a machine shop operated by a man named Sam Skidmoor. Mitch eventually landed a job with Sedcore, a core drilling company in Fairbanks doing gold exploration in Alaska.

In March, I worked with Bernie for a miner named Bob Ault on the Steese Highway, rebuilding an undercarriage on his D9H Caterpillar. It was a valuable experience for me, since our mining operation owned a Cat too. Bernie was an excellent teacher.

Over the winter, I bought an RV so I would have it for our summer mining operation. I set it up at Bob's camp near the rest of the dwellings occupied by his staff. When loneliness got the best of me, I invited Suzy to Alaska since I now had a comfortable place for her to stay. The camp warmly welcomed Suzy and Bob quickly hired her as the camp cook. She was a sight for sore eyes for everyone, and the miners gave her plenty of attention. Just as she was in Poplar, Suzy became the life of every party. Her infectious laugh brightened up the crew's day, and Bob's camp was transformed by her arrival. The cooking was better, and so was the general attitude of everyone there. I also searched for new mining grounds over the winter. I made valuable contacts with other folks who could help us in our search, including Resource Associates of Alaska. They had proved Fish Creek unviable for mining, but had offered claims on Ketchem Creek to Uncle Roger, Doug, and Tim, who were also looking for new ground for the 1982 season. Ultimately, Uncle Roger and Doug decided to mine in Ruby, Alaska, on Long Creek, which had a history of coarse gold and hand mining. It was deep, but the prospecting was good. The Greens offered the Ketchem claims to us, and we went into Fairbanks to talk with Resource Associates about the possibility of Johnson Mining Company setting up at Ketchem Creek. They gave us the chance to prospect mining ground on the creek between the village of Central, Alaska, and Circle Hot Springs.

Trust between a claim owner and a placer gold mine operator is key in the mining business. When we signed the lease, Resource Associates of Alaska required us to contact them before every cleanup so they could have a representative present. It was their way of monitoring our production and taking their ten percent royalty of the total ounces. We contacted them for the first few cleanups, but they never sent someone out to be present. At the end of each season, we presented them their full royalty in gold. Their trust in us was well founded as we always gave them their fair share.

In the spring of 1982, Dad, Mom, Loren, and Deed arrived at the Birch Creek camp. Loren had worked at Cummins in the winter but refurbished a diesel engine in his free time. It was ready to install in the dragline. Loren and Deed also brought someone new to help us—Jim James and his wife, Bobbi, a good friend of Deed's. We all surmised Bobbi was there to make mining and life in Alaska a little more bearable for Deed. During our first year, we had noticed that Deed was the most unhappy at camp, with only her mother-in-law for company during the day. She spent most of her time cleaning her cabin, often leaving the greatest part of the in-camp work to Mom. With Bobbi's arrival, I hoped things would change. However, I remembered a saying my Uncle Roger used to have.

"It's not good to have more than two women at camp; they fight," he said. In the 1982 season, we had four women: Mom, Deed, Suzy, and Bobbi.

Jim was a longtime friend that Loren and I knew from school and Boy Scouts. Jim was an independent contractor and was able to leave his work behind in Superior, Wisconsin, and join us for the summer in Alaska. He and Bobbi brought their own small RV trailer to live in while at the mine.

After arriving at Birch Creek, our first order of business was prospecting on Ketchem Creek for the season. With shovels and gold pans in hand, Loren, Jim, and I drove thirty-five miles to the claims. Resource Associates had dug some holes in the gravel down to the bedrock where miners find the richest gravels. We panned the samples they had left near the digs, and we saw decent color winking back at us. We hurried back to camp.

"How did you do?" Dad asked.

We told him we had seen more gold in our pans at Ketchem

Creek than we had ever seen on Birch Creek. We also thought the area might have kinder weather. We would be at an elevation that would not trap cooler temperatures and precipitation all summer as we had experienced on Birch Creek. It didn't take long for Dad to decide.

"Let's go," he said.

We immediately began preparations to move our operation to Ketchem Creek. We made a sign on a 4 x 8 piece of plywood that read "lowboy wanted" and placed it on the Steese Highway. A few hours later, we had the help we needed. Tim McKay, a local trucker, and heavy hauler by trade, drove by, saw the sign, and stopped. Tim was very small in stature but a real firecracker when it came to moving heavy equipment. He was a gruff little guy with very little patience, but was known to be able to move anything, anywhere in Alaska. Knowing our cash flow challenges, he agreed to move our equipment in two trips for $850, a very fair price. He transported the dragline in one load and the D8 Cat and sluice box in another.

It was a wet spring day when Tim loaded the dragline for the trip over Eagle Summit to Ketchem Creek. He dropped his trailer, and we loaded the complete dragline. Tim then had to back under the trailer with the weight of the dragline. The back of the truck had a ramp that would slide and lift the load onto the rear of his truck. With the wet and slippery conditions, the trailer wouldn't lift. In desperation, Tim rolled on his tire chains and with brute force, launched his truck under the trailer. The frame of his truck twisted and under the load it went, undamaged from the weight. Tim let out what sounded like a growl, as he always seemed angry when he was moving things. After that, we learned it was better for us to stay out of his way when we asked Tim to haul something heavy for us. However, from that day forward, we used him for all our heavy hauling needs. We secured the dragline, and soon it was on its way over Eagle Summit to Ketchum Creek in Central, Alaska. Tim went on to become the "go-to" movers for equipment dealers that needed to reclaim their heavy equipment from failed and abandoned mining operations.

Bernie offered his one-ton truck and flatbed trailer to relocate our cabins. In just a few days, we were setting up our new camp on Ketchem Creek. In true Alaska spirit, caring people and a community of miners that cared about each other came to the aid of our family!

*****

As we suspected, our claims on Ketchem Creek were much better in many ways. It was warmer, sunnier, and drier than our first claims on Birch Creek. We could expect Ketchem temperatures in the 70s most days. On Birch Creek, it had snowed once on the Fourth of July.

The Ketchem Creek mining site was also convenient to the village of Central, Alaska, and the Arctic Circle Hot Springs. Central is a quiet little town with two restaurants, a post office, an airstrip, a grocery store, and a mining museum. When we first started mining in the area, there was a public telephone outside the tavern. Miners would drive for miles from the creeks to order supplies from Fairbanks or call friends and family from that phone.

While we mined on Ketchem, the Hot Springs was in full operation. Circle Hot Springs had an operational swimming pool. After a long, sometimes cold, and wet day, we could relax in the hot pool. It was a destination for locals and tourists, with an old hotel, a saloon, and a restaurant. It was also an oasis for miners in the area for one hundred years. The hotel had rooms we could rent by the hour to take advantage of the jacuzzi tub and have a brief getaway. Even the toilets would flush with hot water.

Our mining site on Ketchem Creek was in a beautiful valley, surrounded by birch, black spruce, and aspen trees. There, the latitude of the land stunted the growth of the trees. They only grew a fraction of the height of the others in their family positioned further south. The smell of the black spruce was powerful, a pine scent like an air freshener in your car, only one hundred times more fragrant. The ground is covered in tundra moss that forms a spongy carpet under your feet.

Wild, low-bush cranberries and blueberries grew in patches among the trees, and Mom picked gallons of them. Because they froze well and kept for months, she would take them back to Wisconsin. She would bake delicious muffins in the winter and would share the tasty berry muffins with her friends over coffee.

There was also a granite outcropping where locals and tourists stopped to view Ketchem Valley. Some would come for the vista, but others would come to view our active mine. "The granite" offered a sweeping view of our land, and we would take our ATVs there at least once a week just to get away from camp for an evening.

Suzy had quit her job with the Wisconsin Department of Transportation and was planning to have a future with me. At the time, I felt it was what I wanted, and I went along with her ideas and plans. I was very busy at the time and focused on the task of mining and creating some kind of financial future for us. Suzy was focused on getting married and had located a Justice of the Peace, in Central.
"It's all done," she said, her brown eyes shining brightly, one day after returning from town. "I've got a Justice of the Peace, and we can get married in Central next week."

With Suzy's plan set, I think I went into panic mode when I heard this. I started asking myself, *is this what I really want?* A little internal voice inside me that never steered me wrong spoke up. *It's not going to work*, it said. I had a history of trusting my instincts and knew my emotions were in response to that little voice. I was twenty-six years old, but it wasn't the right time for me to marry, nor the right woman.

At first, I tried to stay focused on my work and did my best to avoid the upcoming wedding plans, but Suzy wouldn't let me. She may have felt something was wrong, but I waited until the day before our scheduled marriage before I felt I finally had to address the situation.

"Suzy, I'm not ready to get married yet," I told her, the day before the wedding. It wasn't easy to choke out the words, but once I started, I became more and more convinced I was doing the right thing. I explained that I needed some time to be sure what I wanted, and that I would arrange for a trip to Fairbanks and a flight back to Wisconsin for her.

Suzy's normally beautiful brown eyes cut like a knife through me, and she was understandably hurt and angry. As she grilled me about my actions—how I could do it and the unfortunate timing—I honestly didn't have any answers she could readily accept. I just told her I had to do what was right for me.

Our last days together were not very pleasant. As I dropped her off at the Fairbanks airport, she was still furious with me and the situation. Her parting words were very colorful. She also expressed her relief in leaving "bumf&^k" Alaska. Suzy always had a way of putting things that left no questions about how she felt.

Suzy returned to Poplar and stayed with Scott and Holly Lundberg of hardware store fame. She had given up her apartment, and I think she thought I would change my mind before the mining season was over. But it was not to be.

*****

I opened the 1982 mining season on Ketchem Creek by finishing the camp and setting up the mining operation. We used the dragline to dig a hole for the new outhouse and Loren and Jim framed up the shelter. When it was complete, they asked me to backfill and grade around it with the Cat.

As I operated the machine, I got a little too close and nicked the corner of the outhouse. Before I knew what was happening, there was a mighty crunching sound. The entire structure broke apart, and Loren and Jim were standing right there as their creation crashed to the ground in pieces. Anyone who came upon the sight would have surely believed someone set off an explosion! Loren and Jim were quite unhappy with the dozer operator responsible for the destruction in front of them. Then, after helping with reconstruction, I was given a chance to redeem myself and made a second successful attempt to finish the grading and backfilling.

One day we had a visit from one of our neighbors, a colorful character named Joe Vogler. Joe was a roughly distinguished real estate investor and radical who had founded Alaskans for Independence Party and even made unsuccessful runs for office. He made no apologies for openly hating the U.S. government and we once heard him comment that he would like to "kill the last pregnant grizzly bear sow in Alaska." He owned many mining claims, including the claims above us on Ketchem Creek. One day, he stopped at our camp after watching us turn over the ground in search of gold. Over coffee, he told us how impressed he was with our operation and how we were very efficient "dirt movers." Then he asked us where we came from, and of course, we told him we were from Wisconsin.

"You're foreigners," he said, in an unsettling tone.

We found this a curious sentiment since he moved to Alaska from Kansas as a young man. Still, we asked Joe to lease us his mining claims on Ketchem and he refused. Later, we had an issue with him over existing claim lines. Joe was always ready and eager for conflict with anyone. I once made the offhand remark, "Someday someone's gonna murder Joe." Ten years later, Joe disappeared, and his body was found buried in a gravel pit near Fairbanks. His murderer was caught, and Joe's body was exhumed and moved to Dawson City, Yukon, so he could be buried with his wife and not on American soil, just as he wished.

Our new mining claim had been mined in the 1930s by the Engstrom brothers. They had set up their operation when gold sold at a whopping $35 an ounce. During World War II, they shut down and never returned to mine on Ketchem. We were told they moved their equipment to Circle for loading and unloading wartime freight. In those days, they would fill the riffles with mercury because mercury would stick to the gold. It gave the gold a silvery appearance. As we were mining, we came upon some gold with mercury residue. It was like finding a portal to the past.

The historic sluice of the Engstrom brothers still sat near the creek. It would have been nice to preserve it, but we had to replace it with our advanced equipment. We stripped off the overburden and panned down to the pay layer to begin sluicing the first cut. At first, the results were disappointing, but to be expected. We were sluicing previously mined ground, so the yield was less. We were still excited to have a new creek to mine.

After a few days of sluicing, we were washing virgin pay dirt. Gold started accumulating in the sluice box at an unprecedented rate. It was impossible not to get excited, but we were also concerned that we had just hit a hot area and the values would diminish. However, we were quite pleased with the final cleanup from the first cut, knowing some of the gravel we had been washing was tailings from the Engstrom brother's operation.

We began stripping the next cut, an area of ground about 150 x 150 feet. These smaller cuts opened to an easier stripping storage of overburden, but the ground was still completely frozen from the top down. We ripped the black organic overburden and pushed it into the last cut. There was about five or six feet of frozen, barren gravel on top of the pay layer which we removed as it thawed.

We continued to carefully pan as we worked the barren gravel. We needed to see where gold was accumulating enough to justify sluicing. We had to find enough gold to justify the handling of every bit of material several times.

We did well in the second, third, and fourth cuts. Our work gave us hope that we had a viable business that would turn a nice profit. It looked like we had plenty of mineable ground ahead of us to operate for a few years, which was our goal. We worked long hours and days during the summer of 1982 and were rewarded with an income to hold us over for the winter.

As the new guy at the mine, Jim's main job was running the sluice box monitor as the gravel was washed into a slurry and carried down the sluice box. There was lots of work for all of us, including Jim. When we shut down the sluice box after running for a few hours, we would gather around to see our yield. Jim was quick to remind us of "employee's wages" regularly, knowing that we had to pay him along with our current bills before we could keep any profit. It was exciting to see a future in our business because of the rich claim, but we still had to be careful and reinvest in the business if we were to return in 1983.

There were three gold buyers in Fairbanks, and we were working with Oxford at the time. They would stop into our camp every few weeks to pick up gold from us in a helicopter. It saved us a drive to Fairbanks to deliver our gold to the refiner, which we appreciated, but of course, we knew they took the cost of their trip out of our gold deal. On one occasion, as they landed in camp, the velocity of their powerful rotors tore the roof right off our outhouse! We had chuckles all around the camp, grateful that nobody was in there at the time.

*****

Despite the Suzy fiasco, 1982 had been a good year for the Johnson Mining Company. We closed up the mining camp at

Ketchem, looking forward to returning next year. We had plans to expand our operation and bring in a front-end loader to handle dirt more quickly and cheaply than we were able to do with the Cat. I bid the family goodbye and headed to Fairbanks to take care of our final business there before leaving for Wisconsin.

I was in no hurry to return home. I stayed a few days longer in Fairbanks than expected. One day, I was sitting with Mitch and our friend Bob Olson at Bob's home in the hills above Fairbanks. I was thinking about flying to Seattle for a few days to spend time with my Uncle Harlan and his family. I could also then travel to Gresham, Oregon, to visit my brother, Lowell, and his family before heading home. We were all looking at different flight options, and Bob mentioned that he saw Northwest Airlines was running a deal from Fairbanks to Honolulu. If I took the trip and flew from Honolulu to Seattle, I could visit Hawaii for only $50 more than flying direct from Fairbanks to Seattle. I had never been to Hawaii, and it seemed like a "no brainer" after a long summer working seven days a week and snow beginning to fall in Alaska.

After so many good days of gold mining, I thought I had seen my share of treasure for the year. Little did I know that the greatest treasure in my life was right around the corner, just waiting to be discovered.

CHAPTER 5

GREATER THAN GOLD

I made my spontaneous trip to Honolulu from Fairbanks alone. I had no plan for lodging and knew nobody there. I landed and stepped out into the warm, eighty-degree sunshine. I immediately noted the difference between the crisp, fresh air in Alaska and the tropical, humid air on the busy island. Everything was disturbingly different: crowds, colorful shirts, tropical music, sandy beaches, coconuts, and pineapples!

I grabbed a taxi and headed to the Waikiki Beach area, where I knew I could find an inexpensive hotel. I checked in and wandered outside and onto the beach, feeling like a fish out of water. I had planned to spend a week there, relax, and enjoy the warm weather and sights. However, the culture shock was palpable.

After five months of relative isolation in the Alaskan bush, I was walking on crowded streets and approached by strangers asking me to buy drugs or women offering their company for the night. I wasn't interested in any of it. I had about thirteen ounces of gold in my pocket, and I was afraid it would disappear. I only had bulky clothing and didn't even have a swimsuit. So, after a few days of trying to adapt by purchasing a swimsuit, lying on the beach, and returning to an empty hotel room, I was done with Hawaii. I called Northwest Airlines to see if they had earlier flights to Seattle. They told me a seat was available on a direct flight at 1:30 that afternoon. I told them I'd take it.

I was running late to the airport and was the last passenger to head down the jetway. When I walked onto the aircraft, I was greeted by a blond-haired, blue-eyed woman with a ponytail.

"You just made it," she teased, flashing a gorgeous smile.

"Yeah," I replied sheepishly, returning the smile. When our eyes met, I was struck by a feeling that she was someone special I needed to get to know better. She smiled back at me as I walked to the back of the airplane and slid into a seat on the aisle. In my row was a woman about my age. She had obviously been drinking heavily in preparation for the six-hour flight. I was much more interested in the same blond flight attendant who kept passing my seat.

As luck would have it, we were on a Boeing 747 with only 130 passengers onboard. The crew had plenty of time on their hands to do their work and visit with passengers. It wasn't long before my favorite flight attendant came by and asked me if I wanted a beer. I gratefully accepted the offer and noticed her nametag—Linda.

As the flight progressed, I was happy to see that Linda was assigned to serve meals and drinks in my area of the cabin. I could talk to her quite a bit, and I struck up a conversation with her every time she paused near my seat. The woman next to me must have felt Linda was competition because she started trying to get my attention. At one point, she was hanging over me, cigarette in one hand, getting ashes down my shirt. I was about to correct her when Linda strode by.

"Honey, you're going to start him on fire," she said with a disapproving look that stopped the drunk girl in her tracks. Drunk girl returned to her seat, and I dared to wonder if Linda did it purely out of public safety or if she had noticed my interest in her.

Surrounding me were four civilian men who worked for the U.S. Navy and were traveling to Seattle for a project. They were in full celebration mode and kept Linda busy bringing drinks. I enjoyed all my conversations with Linda, as well as the contractors. We were landing in Seattle around 10:30 at night, and I realized I once again didn't have a place to stay. The contractors said they had a rental car and planned to continue the "party" at the Edgewater Hotel, a pricey place on the Seattle waterfront. They asked me to join them, and I agreed since I had no other plans.

As the airplane descended into SeaTac Airport, I realized I had to do something special for Linda. I was so impressed by her kindness and her sweet personality. We had connected on the flight, and I wanted to show my appreciation for all she had done. I reached into my little bottle of gold nuggets and picked out a matching pair of large gold pieces. I shrouded them in a napkin and stopped her as she made one of her last passes through the aisle.

"These are for you," I said, handing her the napkin. "You can make yourself a set of earrings."

Linda accepted the napkin with a look of confusion and curiosity. She didn't unwrap it in the aisle but took it to the flight attendant's area. Later she told me that when she opened the napkin and saw the gold, another flight attendant was looking over her shoulder.

"Linda Lu," the attendant told her, addressing Linda by her nickname, "You've just met yourself a 'gold mine.'"

After we landed, I was intentionally the last person to exit the airplane. As I walked up to the door, there stood the beautiful woman that greeted me when I boarded seven hours earlier. We hadn't known each other for long, but we had become so comfortable with each other it seemed like much longer.

"Thank you for the present," she said, flashing that gorgeous smile again.

All I could do was ask Linda for her phone number. To my surprise, she wrote it on a piece of paper and handed it to me. *This can't be happening*, I thought to myself. I took the paper, stuffed it into my pocket, and promised to give her a call.

I rode with the contractors to the Edgewater and found a room. The plan was to meet them later for a drink in the hotel bar. With hope in my heart, I pulled the precious piece of paper out of my pocket and called the number. I was surprised and delighted when Linda answered the phone.

"Is it too late to meet me for a drink?" I asked.

"No, it's not," she said, a smile in her voice. "But I have to bring my friend, Evon."

Evon was a flight attendant on the same trip and was spending the night at Linda's. She was engaged and getting married in Seattle the following weekend. They met us at the hotel, and we all had a pleasant visit.

At the end of the evening, I walked Linda and Evon to Linda's car. I opened Linda's car door and asked if I could kiss her goodnight. It was our first kiss!

I originally planned to spend three days in Seattle and Gresham before flying back to Poplar, but Evon told me I had to stay and attend her wedding. I wasn't in a hurry to return to Wisconsin. I knew Suzy would be waiting for me to return and try to rekindle our relationship. We had not been in contact since she left Fairbanks, and I knew the pressure would be on once I returned to my place in Poplar. Staying in Seattle was preferable, so I moved from the Edgewater to a cheaper hotel. It turned out that my new hotel was near Linda's apartment by pure coincidence.

Linda had a few days off, so we spent three days seeing the sights of Seattle. We took the Washington State Ferry to Bremerton and explored Pioneer Square. We stopped for a latte at the Starbucks flagship store at the Pike Place Market and strolled the Seattle waterfront. We were on the run and enjoying our whirlwind romance. Suddenly, my parents arrived in Seattle to spend time with my uncle in Lake Forest Park. I carefully asked Linda to come along and meet my parents, assuring her that it needn't be as serious as it sounded. She laughed and agreed to go. We had a lovely dinner with Mom, Dad, Uncle Harlan, and Aunt Arlene at my uncle's house. Mom and Linda immediately hit it off, which was a blessing. Overall, we had a great time, and it was clear that my family liked and accepted Linda. Another great blessing!

Linda offered a place for me to sleep on her couch to save on my hotel fare. I was happy to spend more time with her and took her up on her offer. We spent so much time talking about life and what we wanted. We talked about family, our faith, Linda's flying, and goldmining. Linda reminds me we didn't talk about the experience of camp life, which might have been good preparation for a city girl like her. However, she seemed curious and intrigued by the gold mining lifestyle. She asked me about Suzy, and she told me about her own past too. We were carefully considering a future with each other, and we both knew what we were looking for in a lifetime partner.

However, as all good things must end, Linda had to return to work and fly another trip. I was planning to travel to Portland to spend time with my brother and his family, so Linda suggested I drop her off at the airport and take her car to Portland/Gresham. I could hardly believe her trust in me as I gratefully accepted her offer. It was amazing how close we had become in such a short time.

I dropped her off at the SeaTac Airport, kissing her goodbye and already missing her. Then I drove her car to Gresham and spent a few days visiting my brother Lowell and his family. Linda had baked a box of scrumptious black bottom cupcakes that she wanted me to share with my family. While Lowell and I were away from their house, Lowell's wife, Barb, answered the phone. A woman on the other end asked to speak to me. Barb told her I was out and then, assuming she was Linda, thanked her for the cupcakes.

"What cupcakes?" the woman on the phone asked. It was Suzy, looking for me. I had no idea I was being tracked!

I also spent time in Portland, and Dad met me there. We traded gold for a rubber-tired, front-end loader for the mine on "Machinery

Row." It was reasonably priced but needed some work. We took it to Warren Peterson, a miner we had met in Alaska who operated a machine shop in Woodinville, Washington. We also pulled the engine out and had it rebuilt by an engine shop in Seattle, so it was ready to be shipped to Alaska.

After my trip to Portland, I picked Linda up at SeaTac as she completed her trip. We spent a few more days together in Seattle. Finally, it was time to return to my home in Wisconsin to take care of some unfinished business. Word spread that I was in town, and just as I had feared, Suzy showed up on my doorstep, expressing the desire to salvage our relationship. I told her it was over, which she seemed to accept with genuine regret. Suzy wished me good luck, and in a serious tone she added, "Let me know if it doesn't work out."

Linda and I talked a few times daily while I was in Wisconsin. We discussed the possibility of my moving to Seattle, but she warned me not to come just for her. Neither of us wanted to feel any unnecessary pressure on our relationship. I told her truthfully that I had always thought about living in the Northwest, so Linda found an apartment for me to live in located in the Magnolia neighborhood. I bought a truck to help me move west and tied up loose ends in Wisconsin. Linda flew into Duluth to help me pack up and move.

In March, Linda and I returned to the Hawaiian Islands together. We went to Maui for a week and then spent time in Waikiki for a couple of days. Although we had only known each other for six months, we had talked endlessly, and both felt that we had found what we were looking for in a lifelong partner in each other. Our shared values, comfort level, and Christian faith pointed to a solid future together. So, on a moonlit night in Waikiki, after a delicious dinner on the beach, I turned to Linda and asked her a question. "How would you like to spend the rest of your life with me?"

Immediately, she said yes.

The next day we traveled to Seattle on a Northwest Airlines 747. As Linda was an employee on the flight, we traveled on the upper deck of the airplane with other employees that she knew—Mary from reservations and her husband John, and Susie, another flight attendant. With just the five of us, we had a private engagement party on the flight to Seattle. The crew working the flight made sure we had champagne and hors d'oeuvres, along with a full first-class dinner.

Linda was born and raised in Seattle and was slightly older than me at thirty-four; I was twenty-six. She had also been married briefly, for a period she calls "hardly a marriage." My parents liked Linda the moment they met her. We leapt into our future together, against all odds and conventional wisdom about needing longer courtships and engagements to go the distance. In three short weeks, we planned to wed on April 18, 1983, about six months after we met. And as I write this, we have been married for 40 years. As I said, we just knew it was right.

We had an intimate afternoon wedding at the Chapel at Sand Point Naval Air Station and reception at the Puget Sound Yacht

Club, then spent the night at the Edgewater, where it all began. All of my family flew in for the wedding and supported our union. Everyone was happy for us. Linda's family liked me too.

"You met your match," Linda's dad told her confidently.

It turned out my new father-in-law was from Superior, Wisconsin, but had ended up in Seattle when he joined the Navy. Linda's mom was born in Seattle, but her family later moved to Duluth, where her mom met her dad. Linda still had relatives in both Superior and Duluth. Our fathers had both attended the same high school and were delivered by the same doctor! We marveled at these incredible coincidences as if we had met by fate!

As for Linda, she liked her new family as much as they liked her. I was especially delighted that she got along so well with Mom.

"I couldn't ask for a better mother-in-law," I've heard Linda say many times.

There was only one thing I forgot to tell Linda before we got married. It was a complete surprise when I told her I had been so busy I had forgotten to pay my federal income taxes, which were now due. Linda looked at me in shock and worry, but relaxed when she found out it wasn't a significant amount. She was even a good sport about it and let me write the check from our new joint account!

* * * * *

With the wedding in Seattle, Dad, Mom, Loren, and Deed were prepared to travel to Alaska to mine the 1983 season. Two days later, we loaded up our trucks with supplies. We decided to eat even better this season. We met a good butcher in Seattle called Better Meats and loaded a freezer with beef, pork, and fish to last us in camp over the summer. We also picked up other supplies for the mine too because the prices were much better in Seattle than Fairbanks.

Loren had driven Big Red back to Wisconsin with some heavy parts that needed machining for the dragline, and the plan was to load Big Red onto the Ferry from Seattle to Haines, Alaska. Dad, Mom, and I would drive the highway to Haines Junction and meet Loren and Deed there. Linda had to go to Minneapolis for her annual refresher training with the airline, so I traveled alone in my pickup. Our "honeymoon" would have to wait until after the mining season.

We drove the Alaskan Highway to Haines Junction, Alaska, looking for Loren and Deed. We knew when the ferry docked and when to expect them. We waited, but they never showed up. We started driving toward Haines to see if they had encountered mechanical problems and found him beside the road. The rear end of Big Red had failed. We found a fellow in Haines with an old school bus with a rear end that would work for us. He brought it out to us, and we installed it on the side of the highway so we could continue the trip.

It was always exciting to return to Alaska and open camp, and even better when we found the camp just as we left it. We arrived, ready to work on the D8 and the dragline to prepare them for the season. The first thing we did was get the Cat ready. After a week or so of undercarriage work, it was in shape to start stripping a new cut. While I stripped with the Cat, Loren and Dad installed new parts for the dragline.

Soon, the camp was ready to go, and we were hopeful and excited for the 1983 mining season on Ketchem Creek. However, I knew it would be different this year being a newlywed. It would be Linda's first time at camp. I sure hoped she liked it!

*****

To spend as much time as possible with me, Linda accepted back-to-back Asia flights to accumulate ten days off at a time. It was the high point of the summer for me when she showed up to share my fourteen-foot camper whenever she could.

On her first trip to Ketchem Creek, I combined my trip to Fairbanks to pick her up with an errand to retrieve a set of tracks for the D8 with Big Red. Any time Linda traveled on an airplane during her off-duty hours, she had to dress up and look sharp. As I pulled into the airport to pick her up, she found her white knight's chariot to be Big Red. Carefully, she climbed in good-naturedly.

We had 135 miles to travel to the mine, and 95 miles of the road was gravel. It would not have been a problem except that Big

Red had accumulated a few holes in the floorboards over the years. As we traveled on the gravel road, we soon shared the truck's cab with several clouds of dust. Linda still tells this story at parties!

When I showed her around the mine for the first time, I told her about the dragline and its history. I foolishly mentioned that the old Koehring was an "antique" built in 1948. I realized much too late that 1948 was the year Linda was born.

"Are you saying I'm an antique?" she teased with a glint in her eye. It was one of my first lessons in being a tactful husband!

Linda brought a new addition to our camp—a cat named Scoshi in her little carrier. Linda received Scoshi as a kitten from her neighbor. She named the little orange tabby after the Japanese word for "a little bit." Scoshi was a fun cat who had a mind of her own! As you can imagine, Scoshi felt the call of the wild and wanted to commune with the great outdoors she saw through the RV windows. Even though it had snowed a little that day, it did not discourage her curiosity. I tried to convince Linda that Scoshi would be a happier, more content cat if she understood her environment and that we should let her out to explore. After a bit of persuasion, Linda agreed. She opened the door and watched Scoshi run excitedly outside to adventure.

However, when I returned from work, Scoshi was still not home, and Linda was distraught. I assured her the cat would be fine, but when it came time for bed, Scoshi was still nowhere in sight. Linda was now angry with me, and I realized I may have overestimated

Scoshi's survival skills. After all, we resided in the Alaska bush, and Scoshi could easily be gone for good as prey for an owl, eagle, wolf, lynx, or other predators among us.

In the morning, we heard a "meow" coming from outside. We looked out the window, and there was Scoshi, returning to the camper, looking hungry but unscathed. We knew the cat would undoubtedly now have a new appreciation for its inside home! We assumed she hid for the night under the brush and snow. Scoshi must have learned an important lesson that night because she didn't ask to venture out into the Alaska wild by herself again. Scoshi didn't like camp life much, so she became a seasoned traveler. Linda took her back and forth to Seattle during the summer.

The RV became our honeymoon suite, and Linda affectionately called it our "Candlelight Condo." We fell into a comfortable domestic rhythm, pausing occasionally to work through some hiccups. For example, Linda would cook breakfast most mornings while I dressed and got ready for work. Because the RV had a very narrow walkway through the kitchen area, we had to take great care passing through. One morning, I learned a hard lesson while side-stepping past the stovetop. Linda had bacon frying, and my exposed posterior landed squarely on the sizzling frying pan. OUCH! After that, I learned to navigate the RV in pants and move frying pans out of the way!

Linda had not grown up in a family that camped, so the entire lifestyle was new. She made some innocent mistakes in those first few months as she learned how the conveniences of the big city were unavailable in the bush. For example, camp life meant a limited water supply, as we had to haul it from a water source with our pickup truck. One morning, I left for work after filling our water tank to the top. I came home after a long day and was looking forward to a nice, relaxing shower. I turned the water on, and only a sad, few drips trickled out of the spout. Linda had been home all day and had used up all the water in the tank! If I wanted a shower, I had to haul more water!

Then there was the time when she needed to get ready for a return to work. She was required to dress up in full hairstyle and makeup. We had a 4K Onan diesel generator behind a berm that supported the fuel tank and usually provided enough power for the whole camp. As usual, Linda plugged in her curling iron, iron, hair dryer, and other small appliances to look beautiful for her trip. The poor generator gasped and bellowed black smoke, trying to keep up with Linda's power demands. According to the legend, Dad saw the smoke and knocked on our door.

"What in tarnation are you doing in there?" he shouted to Linda.

"I'm just getting ready," she replied innocently.

On some evenings, Linda and I would head to the Artic Circle Hot Springs Hotel in Central to get away from the camp. In the placer gold mining business, having a resort like this within eight miles of where we were mining was an incredible luxury. Most mines, like Birch Creek, are much further from civilization.

Next to the lodge there was a laundromat, ice-cream parlor, small gift shop, and a large greenhouse that supplied the hotel with fresh vegetables. The greenhouse sold the vegetables to the hotel first and then to the public. Sometimes we could bring some back to camp. Even the freshest Fairbanks produce wasn't the best quality, so Linda often bought us a suitcase of fresh produce from Pike Place Market in Seattle when she joined us at camp.

There was also a public phone in a private booth inside the hotel. During the first few months of our marriage, in the days before satellite and cell phones, I called her from the booth when we were apart. Linda was in Honolulu then, and each call cost fifty dollars, so we only spoke twice. We were grateful to have such an oasis nearby, but shortly after we sold our interest in the Ketchum Creek mine, the resort went into disrepair, and has been reduced to a mere memory.

Sometimes we would drive thirty-five miles from Central into Circle City. Circle City was on the banks of the Yukon River and was another historic village at the end of the Steese Highway. The Yukon River was the main attraction of Circle, and the area was a makeshift social hub for many of our miners.

The miners in the Circle Mining District organized an annual picnic in August. The picnic was a nice break from the seven-day-per-week grind and a chance for the miners to get together and enjoy time together. It was a day to meet new people in the business and for the Fairbanks suppliers to network in Circle Hot Springs. Among the miners, everyone had the same dream, and was willing to help each other achieve it. Just as new friends helped us, the Johnson Mining Co. would give advice, do small favors, and assist others where possible. It was a true community of friendly and helpful friends.

Bernie and Connie Karl hosted an annual pig roast for a few years, including a potluck gathering of all the local miners at Bernie's Camp near Gold Dust Creek. Bernie supplied the pig and invited everyone from the district and Fairbanks who was willing to come.

Bernie had been in Alaska since the pipeline days. I regularly used the skills he had taught me while working for him, like welding and repairing the Cat. Bernie was always there to offer advice during our years in Alaska. As I write this, Bernie is still there with many irons in the fire. He owns K&K Recycling and Chena Hot Springs Resort in Fairbanks. During the fall and winter months, Chena Hot Springs is a destination for travelers from around the world to observe the Northern Lights. Bernie augmented his resort's amenities by using the hot springs water in geothermal applications to do many different things. His crowning achievement is the creation of the Aurora Ice Museum at the resort. The ice museum stays twenty-five degrees year-round thanks to Bernie's patented absorption chiller. It's quite a hit in the summertime!

The Circle district socials were where we met Freddy Wilkinson, whose grandfather was one of the stampeders of the Gold Rush of 1898. Mining was in Freddy's blood, and in 1984, he moved his operation to Ketchum Creek on Joe Vogler's claims, just above us.

Freddy is a humble, quiet man who has become a legend in Alaska and continues to mine to this day.

We also met Stan Gelvin, who mined with his dad, Ed, on Greenhorn Creek and Crooked Creek. Stan passed his knowledge down to his son, Jimmy, who is still mining on Crooked Creek. Stan and his dad are pilots and had an airstrip behind their homes in Central, Alaska, to fly their airplanes. Stan had a Stearman biplane and took me for a ride with him one evening. A Stearman is a WWII biplane that was used by the Army and Navy to train pilots. He harnessed me in tightly to demonstrate how he could do an inside loop. He was an excellent pilot who gave me a birds-eye view of our claims and mining operation. Upon seeing it, I swelled with pride and gratitude to be able to enjoy a successful livelihood in such a beautiful place. Stan took Linda for a ride the same evening, but she declined the experience of the inside loop!

Stan's wife, Andrea, became a good friend to Mom. Unfortunately, Stan and Andrea went their separate ways in 1986. However, Phyllis and Andrea's bond was deep, rooted in faith, and they were there for each other in life's most difficult moments. Andrea had severe anxiety about flying but conquered her fears by taking lessons and eventually buying an airplane. She is a true winner and remains a special friend of ours today.

When Doug and Uncle Roger started mining, they worked beside Eddy and Betty Dugas from Silver Bay, Minnesota. Together they mined claims on Sourdough Creek at 66 Mile Steese Highway.

After the first year, they dissolved the partnership, and the families started independent operations. We quickly became mutual friends with the Dugas family, and they mined for several years in the Circle mining district before retiring.

Linda enjoyed the social time of our mining operation, but she also willingly pitched in with the work. When we moved to Ketchum Creek, we discovered the laundromat at the Arctic Circle Hot Springs just eight miles away. Mom and Deed were elated to say goodbye to laundry using the cumbersome, manual Maytag. Solving the laundry hardship made life easier for everyone in camp.

For groceries and supplies, we took turns driving. Sometimes, the women made the 135 miles to Fairbanks together to pick up groceries. There were also emergency trips to pick up equipment parts after breakdowns to get us back into production.

We noticed that when the fresh groceries came out, Deed would bring her week-old fruits and vegetables to Mom's trailer for us to finish and take the fresh produce from Fairbanks home for her and Loren to eat. Once again, we bit our lip and kept up the "peace at any price" philosophy to avoid conflict. Deed's "me first" attitude was challenging throughout our mining years.

*****

Our gold production went well in 1983. The rubber-tired loader was excellent for feeding the sluice box and gave us better use of the

Cat. We could stack pay dirt for the loader and park the Cat or use it for other necessary mining work while the sluice box was running. Jim James was with us to run the loader for the summer and was efficient and experienced. Fortunately, the ground was shallow, and we were washing an impressive square footage of bedrock.

We still had the challenge of separating the gold from the black sand. So, we invested in a Willen Jig to process our cleanups and break down the volume of concentrates. This saved time on the gold wheel, which cleaned the gold well enough to sell to the refiners. It was time-consuming, but Mom was the most efficient at it. She never complained when she finished a large batch, only for us to bring her more to process.

During sluicing, we would rake and loosen the dirt in the riffles after we shut down the box or before we started it up. One morning, our raking revealed a beautiful, imperfectly shaped, three-ounce nugget in the nugget trap. It was the largest we had ever caught and was very exciting as we all took turns showing it to our wives. It looked exactly like an unassuming heavy piece of quartz interlaced with bands of gold. We figured the rock contained about two ounces of gold, hosted by quartz. We could have extracted the gold from the nugget by crushing it, but we chose to keep it in its natural state. Such nuggets are extremely rare and can bring a premium price if you decide to sell them. However, we thought the nugget so unique we saved it. We still have it to this day!

At the end of the season, we were very pleased with our

summer's work and production. We did so well that in the fall, Mom and Dad purchased a Class C motorhome to enjoy one of their favorite activities in the off-season more easily —camping. They permanently left their fifth wheel in Alaska, intending to use the motorhome during winter months to visit family and vacation in the warm weather. There was a new excitement for them ahead to enjoy the coming retirement years.

*****

For Linda and me, any inconveniences or drawbacks from our summers at camp melted away during the winters together. I would fly with her on her trips, and we spent beautiful days in places like Hawaii, or winter adventures, like skiing in Austria. Back home, I kept busy remodeling our home in Seattle and building furniture. I missed her when she was gone and would send flowers to her hotel.

Honestly, 1983 was the first of many challenging mining years for Linda. The commute to Alaska wasn't fun after flying for her job. In the winters, I was itching to travel, but the last thing she wanted to do was step aboard an airplane on her days off. We did compromise and take many vacations though, and I was grateful to get out of town and be with her someplace special.

For me, 1983 was the year I found Linda, a treasure greater than gold. I had met my match, and she had even survived her first summer at camp like a champ. Now, we turned our attention to starting a family and preparing for any challenges ahead.

CHAPTER 6

CHANGING TIMES

The mining years on Ketchem Creek were the best we ever had. We were in predictable and consistent mining ground. The overburden was shallow, which was typical in the Circle mining district, and we usually only had to remove six feet of frozen organic black muck and the six feet of frozen gravel underneath.

However, our operation was changing with the need to comply with new and more stringent water quality requirements from the EPA. We were now required to have a complete recirculatory system for our sluicing, using water from our own settling pond. Every miner was required to build a settling pond to reuse their water. Ketchem had a much smaller drainage than Birch Creek, but we were still able to create a water reservoir for our sluicing needs.

We hired the son of one of the pilots for Northwest Airlines that Linda had flown with to work with us in 1984. Denny Cooper was a good worker and very skilled in welding and fabricating. He also had experience mining in a town called Chicken, Alaska. He brought along his wife, Julie, who enjoyed the mining life. With a third woman in camp full-time, teams formed, and Mom was often the odd man out against Deed and Julie.

The flight attendants at Northwest Airlines had filed a class action lawsuit because men were given private quarters on layovers and women were required to share rooms. Linda's piece of the settlement was $13,000 and she used $8,000 of it to buy a roomier, more comfortable, twenty-eight-foot Coachman camper for us when we lived at the mine. I took it as a good sign that Linda was okay with the mining life, and she was willing to invest in our mine and our future. I also took it as a good sign that our marriage was going well!

We had decided to add a vibrating grizzly feeder for the season for faster separation of gold from the gravels. The machine was designed to separate material quickly, reduce our water volume requirement, and remove the need for a man to wash the pay dirt in the head box of the sluice. It was an unwieldy piece of equipment that we knew would help us easily comply with the new regulations. We bought it in Kent, Washington, and shipped it to Anchorage on the barge system. Once again, we hired steadfast Tim McKay to transport it to the mine.

Denny and Loren were a great team. They spent time building screen decks under the grizzly bars to classify the material even more efficiently. They installed an inch-and-a-half screen and a five-eighths screen under the grizzly bars. Anything smaller than five-eighths of an inch dropped onto a steel slick plate and was sluiced down the box. Thanks to the customized grizzly, ninety percent of the gold was stopped within the first four feet of the sluice box and the larger rocks and gravel were discharged from the feeder to circumvent the sluicing process altogether. Loren and Denny also built a water manifold and plumbing system to wash the material through the operation. With very little tweaking, we improved our recovery yield over previous years while satisfying all EPA requirements.

While Loren and Denny were setting up the wash plant, Dad and I were working on the other equipment and stripping our first cut for the season. When we were ready to start sluicing, we set up the monster grizzly feeder and decided our only option to feed it was with the dragline. Easier said than done!

On the first cut, Loren and I practically buried the feeder trying to drop the pay dirt into our relatively small target—the 8x8 hopper from seventy feet of boom. We decided to take twenty feet out of the boom, reducing it to fifty feet. Our feeding then went much better, with much less spillage.

However, we didn't realize that when we set up the feeder, it leaned to one side and the bearings ran dry on one end of the two large eccentric shafts. As a result, the bearings failed, which led to a major repair to replace them on one side. Unfortunately, it was the beginning of several more bearing failures. Some contaminated oil in the housing harmed the bearings on the opposite end of the shafts. We had to stop and make some quick repairs to continue producing. Eventually, though, we needed to stop and give the entire machine an extensive cleaning. We pulled the bearings from both sides, thoroughly cleaned the housing, and replaced all four bearings.

We used our loader to pull tailings which we used to build and grade nice roads. With our new and improved plant, we were able to sluice about 150 yards per hour between Dad, me, Loren, and Denny. We felt very efficient and sluiced quickly, with impressive yields, all through the long summer days.

Linda continued to brighten the camp when she arrived from Seattle to spend her days with us. She would often bring the fresh produce we craved, neatly packed in her suitcases. She was a great team player and a joy to have in camp. She and Mom were a dynamic duo and Linda helped her with the work as much as she could when she was there. They had become great friends and would lean on each other through thick and thin.

The cleanups were hefty that year. We would bring Mom the gold to clean almost weekly and many times she was still working on the last cleanup. The black sand on Ketchem was tough and the gold wheel had to run practically every day, all day. During the evenings we could be found hand picking some of the coarser gold that was impossible to clean with the wheel. We would sit at Mom and Dad's table, picking and talking. Looking back, we hardly noticed the work because the company was so good. I just remember relaxing, drinking coffee, and taking a break to enjoy Mom's baked goods. Those were quiet evenings with surreal nighttime sunshine and fun conversations. 1984 was also the year we approached our unfriendly neighbor, Joe Vogler, to lease some of his claims. I was in Fairbanks the day Loren, Dad, and Joe were walking claim lines through the brush. Loren told me Joe was a tough guy to follow. He carried a .44 Magnum revolver on his hip and leapt like a rabbit through the brush, faster than expected for his years and physical condition. The claims would have been a nice addition to the ground we had on Ketchem Creek, but Joe would not lease to us "foreigners."

Not only non-Alaskans, but non-experienced folk tried to goldmine in those days. The Robinson crew was a group of interesting characters who came to the Circle mining district from Los Angeles, California. They were led by an attorney who was rumored to have a bit of a shady history. I have no evidence for some of the rumors I heard about their dishonesty, but my experiences of the Robinson crew only revealed they didn't know what they were doing!

The group of novice miners worked on Portage Creek but came to our camp on several occasions to borrow plumbing parts or tools. We helped in every way we could. One day, we visited their operation. We watched in wonder, shaking our heads about their methods and wondering how they were going to make money. They had a D8H bulldozer they were using to push their pay dirt across the creek in a slurry. Most miners understand when gold is in contact with water, it drops quickly to the bottom and is harder to recover. Pushing the slurry across the creek was a good way to lose the gold in the pay dirt.

When they lifted the blade on their bulldozer, we noticed the changeable cutting edges were worn right into the bolt holes that held them in place. They were slowly destroying the part of the equipment known as the frog, used to support the cutting edge. We could tell it would have to be replaced soon to keep operating. The frog either needed a major welding repair or they would have to purchase a new frog, remove the damaged one, and weld on a new one. Either way, it would be time-consuming and expensive for their operation. It was obvious the crew didn't check their heavy equipment and maintain it daily like miners should do.

I also heard that once they had parked their rubber-tired loader without setting the parking brake. The bucket was left in the air, allowing the machine to roll forward. The loader bucket found its way into the crew's Ford pickup truck and smashed out the windshield and back window. I met the six of them on the road one day, driving the pickup truck with no front window, no back window, and their hair blown straight backwards by the wild, unblocked wind. They stopped for a chat and confirmed the story of the runaway loader and how they had to raise the pickup truck with a loader to shake the teeth of the bucket loose from the truck. I don't know if they ever made a profit from their operation, but they certainly gave the Circle mining district some good tales!

We started looking for a larger Cat to get ahead on our stripping during the next year. Our favorite dealer, NC Machinery in Fairbanks, had a D10L bulldozer on rental to another miner. We were next in line to get it on Ketchem when we were informed that the other miner had decided to purchase the machine. We were offered the option to rent a D9L bulldozer out of Fairbanks. We opted to try the machine for a 250-hour rental period and were able to get a large area stripped ahead for the 1985 season. We were also able to move the frozen black muck for much less cost per yard with the bigger machine and also increase our gold production. When we finished, we had it hauled back to Fairbanks. It was one of the best decisions of the season!

*****

The following year we had a new hire helping us at camp—Dale, Deed's brother. Deed and Loren, who were still childless, had been on a list to get a baby girl from Colombia. It was now 1985, and with each passing year, our family could see that Deed was more and more unhappy to be there.

We decided to move our operation downstream to start another pass upstream. The streak of pay dirt was wide, and we were able to mine the valley floor from limit to limit. Loren brought the dragline down and dug a drain in the frozen gravel. It would take a couple attempts to dig the drain as it thawed. While Loren was digging drainage, we were stripping the new cut. We were also nearby to help Loren rip through the frozen material. The ground was deeper as we moved downstream. It became too deep for our Cat, but the machine was all we had.

Loren was in close contact with Deed with phone calls from the Hot Springs Hotel, expecting to hear from Colombia that their daughter was ready to be placed. We had just finished digging the drain and stripping the cut when Loren got the word. It was time to go to Colombia and bring home their baby girl! Loren needed to head back to Wisconsin right away. Linda arranged for first class, roundtrip tickets from Duluth to Miami with family passes, from where they left for South America. We said goodbye to Loren and wished them luck, happy that the couple was getting their heart's desire.

While he was gone, we set up the plant and started sluicing. We were getting a lot of rain. The creek was rising a bit, but we were grateful to have higher water. The second day, we were sluicing when we noticed black clouds over Ketchem Dome, one of the mountains above our valley. Back then, there were no radio weather reports or other means of getting weather forecasts. The sky was our only clue to impending weather on Ketchem Creek, but the appearance of the clouds didn't concern us. We shut down for lunch without a clue what was about to happen.

When we returned to the cut, we saw a torrent of water streaming down the mountainside, heading right at us. It had already breached the dike we had built to hold the creek back. We heard the sounds of rock and dirt grinding down into our cut, and helplessly watched as the torrent attempted to reclaim the valley floor.

All of a sudden, we spied one of the water pumps we had been using to dewater the cut, on one side of the newly created river now running through our cut. Dale quickly grabbed a chain and jumped on the three-wheeler we used for transportation around the mine. I knew he was planning to bring a chain to the pump so I could pull it out of danger with the Cat. I jumped on the dozer but watched in dismay from my seat as the raging water toppled Dale's three-wheeler and submerged it, leaving the three wheels to surface above the current, bobbing aimlessly in the water.

Dale scrambled up from under the three-wheeler and had the presence of mind to grab the chain before it could disappear underwater. He continued to cross the swift current, wading waist deep across the river until he got to the pump. I met him on the other side after plunging through the water with no difficulty in the Cat. I inched my way up to where Dale stood, and he hooked the chain to the pump and my blade. With a mighty snort of the Cat's engine, the pump dislodged, and I lifted it out of harm's way to a safer, higher location.

For a moment, Dale and I stood and surveyed the damage helplessly. It was considerable. For the next two days, we watched the river run through our cut, washing eight feet of gravel in place of the eight feet we had spent days stripping away the weeks before. We had to start over. We had no choice. We would also have to create a new settling pond. Fortunately, we managed to get the three-wheeler dried out and running again and the pump we saved remained fully operational. A few bright spots in an otherwise tragic event!

We worked hard to divert the creek into our bypass once more and start re-digging the drain and stripping the cut. We didn't find out what had caused the flooding until a few days later. A mountaintop storm had caused a deluge into the pond of another miner on Holdem Creek above us. The water breached the sides of his pond, adding the stored water there to join the already large amount of runoff from a bad storm atop the mountain. We had been the innocent victims of a domino effect from a weather event that we couldn't have foreseen. It never even rained at our location in the valley.

The owner of the mine explained the situation and apologized to us for what had happened. He, too, had to start over with much of his work for that season. We all learned a lesson to fortify our ponds against unseen flooding risks. Unfortunately, it was another task we had to complete with Loren being gone and our operation a man short.

*****

Loren and Deed were away from camp for about a month. After retrieving their new daughter, they flew back home to Wisconsin and stayed a month. Then they joined us at camp and introduced us to the new addition to their family, Anna Maria. She had been born in January and was six months old when she first arrived at camp. It was fun to have a little one with us and we delighted in making her smile and seeing her cute dark curls and beautiful brown eyes.

Then, we didn't see much of Deed and Anna. She kept to her cabin most days and continued family dinners alone with Loren when he returned from the mine. The heavy work of gold cleaning and errands was left to the other women at the camp.

It took us three weeks to get the washed in-gravel removed and start sluicing again while Loren was away. By the time he returned, we were ready to jump back in production. He was amazed at our flood story and helped us recreate the pond with safety measures in place against nature's fury and neighborly pond failures.

Linda and I also wanted to start a family during the Ketchem Creek years, but after three miscarriages, we were beginning to feel hopeless. It was especially difficult for Linda. One day, I sat down with Dad to discuss it, and mentioned the possibility of adoption for us.

Dad looked at me. Without hesitation he asked, "What are you waiting for?" It was all the encouragement I needed. Soon afterward, Linda and I decided to move forward with the adoption process.

*****

As the 1985 season drew to a close, a friend of the family's son contacted me and asked me to transport a box back to Washington State for him. He brought the sealed box to the mine, and I agreed to take it south when I drove home at the end of the season. Because I trusted him, I didn't question the contents in the box. He was in the Coast Guard, so I figured he had a solid understanding of Canadian custom law. A few days before I left, his parents came to the mine looking for me. They asked for the box and told me there was a handgun inside. They didn't want me to get in trouble for gun smuggling across the Canadian border!

I had flashbacks to my first year returning from Alaska and traveling through Canada with Mitch and Scott Lundberg. Scott had flown to Fairbanks to drive back with us to Wisconsin. We planned to take the scenic, long way home traveling first to Anchorage, Homer, and then to Haines, Alaska, to meet the Alaska Ferry. We planned to take the ferry to Prince Rupert, British Columbia, then travel the highway to Wisconsin.

When I left the mine, I badly wanted to take my Ruger 357 Magnum back to Wisconsin. Of course, it was illegal to transport a handgun through Canada. I was supposed to send it from the authorized gun dealer in Alaska to an authorized gun dealer in Wisconsin. However, I thought I would save time and expense and instead take it with me. In the back of my truck, I carried a welder. The machine had a shroud on top of the engine, and I thought it looked like an unassuming hiding place for my gun. I wrapped the Magnum in a towel and hid it inside the cover of the welder, under the shroud. I replaced the cover and thought I would be fine with the transport.

When I entered Canada at Beaver Creek, I was at the wheel. The customs agent on duty was a woman about my age. She asked the typical questions about alcohol, tobacco and then the clincher.
"Sir, do you have any guns with you today?" she asked.

"No," I answered quickly.

She had brown piercing eyes that seemed to see through me.
"Sir, do you have any guns?" she repeated, looking at me in disbelief.

I denied having any guns with me, but she persisted with the gun questions. She even took a visual scan of my truck bed, which was fully loaded with supplies from camp. My heart jumped when she took a look around the truck bed and walked past the welder. "We're moving back home from our mining season in Alaska," I said, offering a simple explanation for all the stuff in the truck. I was relieved when she gave up.

"Okay, go ahead, have a good trip," she finally said.

I breathed a sigh of relief. On that day I learned a lesson at border crossings. I would never risk breaking their firearm laws again. I could have lost my gun, my gold, the truck, and even been prohibited from entering Canada in the future.

Our friend's parents had driven the 135 miles to save me from illegally transporting their son's handgun through Canada. I do think their son knew it was illegal, and maybe customs would not have searched the box. However, if they had, I would have been considered responsible. Ignorance of the gun laws was no excuse with Canadian customs! I heartily thanked them for their efforts. They would have felt bad if I had been caught and I certainly didn't need to be banned from driving Canadian highways!

We typically had handguns in camp for our own protection, but we never tried to bring them back to the U.S. again after my experience through Canadian Customs. Most of the time, we just left them in camp. While that may have been risky, I am happy to say that in all our years at the mine, we never had a break-in at camp.

Even without guns, Canadian border checks made our entire family nervous because we never really knew what to expect and how they would treat us from year to year. When Dad and I pulled our fifth wheel through Canada into Alaska, Mom placed a *Focus on the Family* magazine by Dr. James Dobson in a drawer right by the door. The customs agent took two steps inside the trailer and pulled the drawer open. He picked up the magazine, took one look at us and said, "I've seen enough, you can go." We proceeded on our way with a big "thank you" to Mom!

During the winter of 1985, Linda and I had a chance to spend a few days with Mom and Dad in Florida. We told them that we had started the adoption process, and we were excited to see where this new adventure would lead. Sitting across their kitchen table, we had plenty of laughs with Mom and Dad; this time, without hand-picking the gold. It was nice to see them so happy doing what they had dreamed of for so many years. We were grateful for the time together, especially not knowing what lay ahead.

* * * * *

Returning to Ketchem Creek in 1986, we decided not to hire any help. Dad, Loren and I were on the machines, operating the business as a trio, just as we once had in the woods near Poplar. Mom continued doing our gold cleanups.

It was another good year for us. We had a good area opened so stripping went well, even with our smaller crew. We had cut a prospect trench on the right limit of the valley. At the time we were not sure if gold would be found there, but after sluicing a bulk sample, we found the ground was mineable.

Upon hearing this, Dad would rise at five o'clock in the morning to strip a new cut of about five-hundred feet long by two-hundred feet wide. I would wake to the noise of him stripping away at the cut. Loren and I would eat our breakfast and head down to start sluicing. Dad would take a break, have breakfast with Mom, and return later.

As we mined on our upper claims, we found the gold was thinning out a bit. We were still profitable but not as much as before. One day, late in the season, I was on the Cat stripping and Loren and Dad were setting up the water system so we could begin sluicing. Loren and Dad were both pulling on a section of the six-inch hose that fed water to the wash plant. Suddenly, I noticed Dad was having some problems in his chest. I still remember the odd sight of him resting near the hose. It concerned him as well as the rest of us. He decided to take a day and go into Fairbanks to see a doctor for a heart evaluation. When he returned, he said it was a fibrillation problem and the doctor advised seeing his cardiologist when he returned to Wisconsin.

We finished the cut and moved our operation down to the new one Dad had been stripping. We set up the plant and started sluicing the poor paying gravel off the top of the cut. It was a good-sized cut and still frozen deep into the gravel, but we had a good start on it for next season. We were all tired, and I know Dad wasn't feeling well but didn't want to be the one to quit. The three of us sat down on the side of a gravel pile to have a cup of coffee and talk.

"What do you guys want to do?" he asked.

It was September 15 and there wasn't much time left before the snow would begin to fall.

Loren and I answered simultaneously.

"Let's go home."

Three days later, we were out of camp and on our way home.

*****

It had been a good season on Ketchem Creek. I returned home to Seattle and Linda. Loren began building a large garage onto his house in South Range, Wisconsin, just outside of Poplar. He was hoping to get the trusses up and the roofing on before the first winter snow, so he asked for my help. I flew back to Wisconsin to help Loren and Dad close in the garage before winter hit.

Dad dropped me off at the airport when it was time to fly back to Seattle. As we said goodbye, I saw a tear in his eye. Dad never cried, but he had been working with the doctors regarding his heart issues and he was worried. I never dreamed it would be the last time I would be with him.

When I returned home, Dad called and told me he was calling all of us to tell us that he had scheduled a valve replacement for Tuesday, November 25. I could hear in his voice how concerned he was about the operation itself, as well as the way it might impact his remaining quality of life. I tried to give him what little comfort I could. He was tough, and I was sure he would pull through.

As the surgery day grew closer, Mom and Dad prepared to host the entire family for Christmas 1986 in Poplar. The only problem was their water well was still limited. It only produced two quarts a minute, which wasn't enough to support the expanded family under one roof during the Christmas holidays. Mom and Dad asked Bud Long, a local well driller, to sink a new well on the property on the far side of the driveway, approximately two hundred feet from the house. However, Dad first lined up his friends Conrad Johnson and Wally Johnson to dig a trench from the new well site to the house.

On Thursday, November 20, they arrived to help Dad dig the trench. Dad was tired but wanted to assist as he could. He was cutting a strap from the polyethylene water pipe for installation when he collapsed on the ground. It was the last thing he ever did. Conrad and Wally tried CPR, but he was gone. He never regained consciousness.

Dad's death was a complete shock to the family. Linda and I flew back to Poplar to attend the funeral with the rest of my siblings. Despite his heart problems, Dad was only sixty-one and in excellent shape from years of physical work. It just seemed impossible he wasn't with us anymore. We had lost an irreplaceable person in our family, and a partner in the mining operation.

The night of the funeral, Linda and I stayed at the home place. I walked outside to be alone for a few minutes. The finality of this day had left me with an indescribable, empty feeling. I turned north and was surprised to be greeted by the northern lights; aurora borealis, resplendent in the dark sky. In a village as far north as Poplar, so small that light pollution never interferes with stargazing, it wasn't the first time I had seen the northern lights. It was November and they were sometimes visible between September through March. That night, I couldn't help feeling that the ethereal green band that mingled and danced across the north horizon was no coincidence. It was more than an atmospheric miracle. In that private moment between me and the world, it was a divine sign from Dad that we would all be okay.

During that fall and winter, I made several trips back to Poplar from Seattle to help Mom adjust to the new chapter in her life. Dad had a 40x60 foot garage, filled to the brim with tools and materials that had to be distributed elsewhere. I was also in Poplar when Bud Long returned to finally drill the well. I will never forget the day he told us that the new well was good for twenty gallons of fresh, soft water per minute. Mom sat down at the table in disbelief and cried. After raising her family with two quarts a minute for so many years, now she had an unlimited supply of water. Connections were made from the well to the house, and all was set for the family to be together at Christmas.

The entire Johnson clan gathered in Poplar for Christmas and Mom was able to see all her children and grandchildren. It was a difficult holiday but a necessary time of healing. We were grateful to be together, and it was so good for Mom to be surrounded by her family.

Despite losing our fearless leader, the unspoken intention of me, Loren, and Mom to return to mining in 1987 hung in the air. She loved her days at camp, and one of her best friends, Andrea, would be there to help her through what promised to be an emotionally difficult time. I was happy when she eventually voiced her desire, and we looked at each other with sad smiles, knowing the mine would never be the same without Dad.

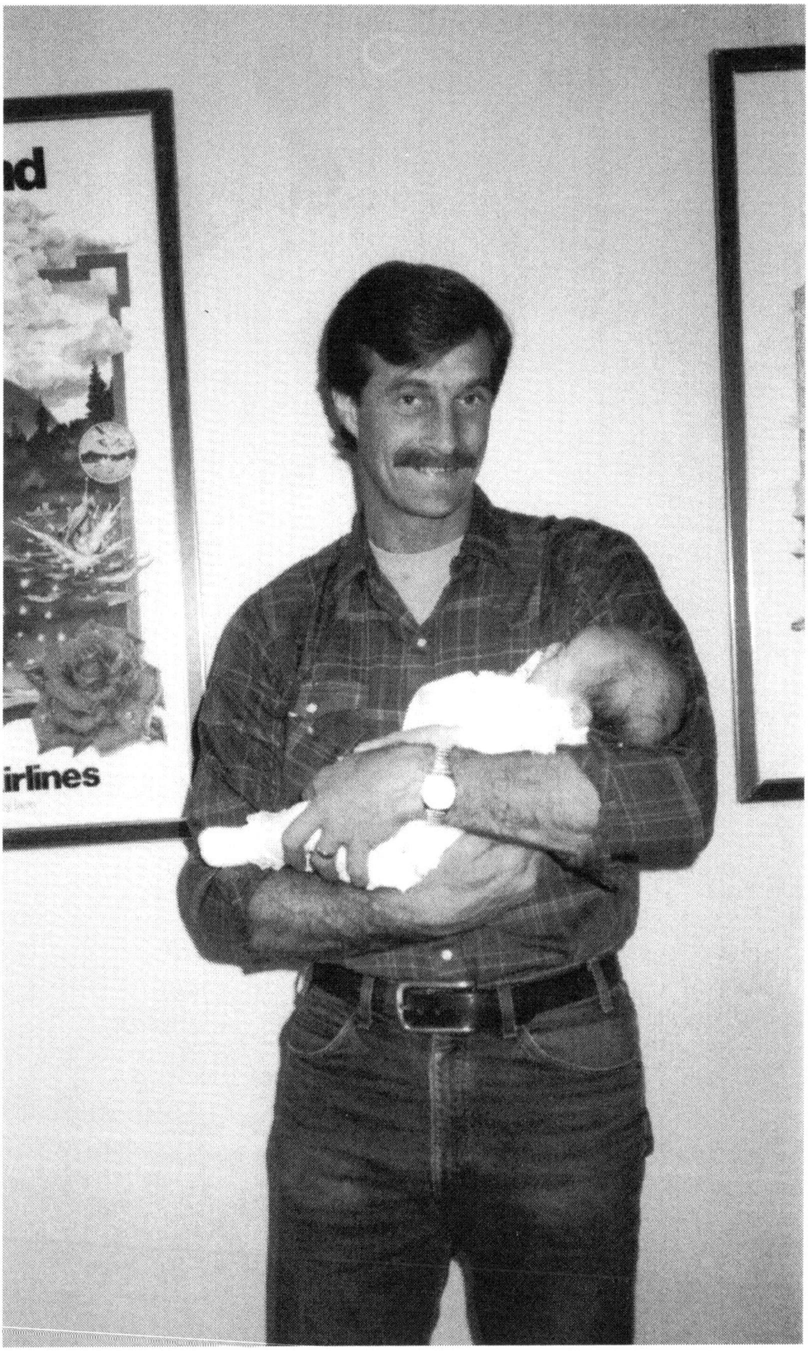

CHAPTER 7

STORM CLOUDS GATHER

We knew returning to Ketchem Creek for the 1987 season without Dad would be difficult. His absence left a huge void in our camp and operation. We assumed Mom as our partner and split the annual profits three ways. It only seemed fair for all her hard work all summer. Plus, we needed her just as much, if not more, than the previous years. She was our gold cleaner, cook (when our wives were away), and bookkeeper, which were all extremely important to us and our success.

Typically, when we arrive at camp in the spring, the first thing we do is maintenance on the equipment. During the season, we only shut down to do repairs if immediately necessary. Otherwise, we wait until spring when it is warmer, and we have the parts to do the repairs. In 1987, it was an adjustment for Loren and me to work on a machine at camp without Dad, and the first of many reminders we would have throughout that first year without him.

In 1987, we brought up Bob Johnson from Lake Nebagamon, Wisconsin. Bob was a single guy and one of the sons of D.L. Johnson Construction, where I had worked. D.L. Johnson had shut down their business, so Bob decided to try something new and join our adventure.

Together we began sluicing the cut Dad had stripped the previous summer, and we had already prepared for mining. We were surprised with the amount of gold we saw coming out of the gravel, but we had no idea how good it was going to be when we reached bedrock.

The cut's bedrock was different from the usual decomposed granite that presented as light-colored sand that was flat as a tabletop. Instead, we hit rock comprised of decomposed chunky schist, or metamorphic rock with large, sheet-like slabs. The bedrock started as small, fractured pieces, about two-inch square, but as we dug deeper, the chunks became more prominent and contained more gold. When we sluiced the bedrock, the gold was even better. We were relieved and happy to learn precisely where to find more gold!

The only problem was processing the rock; the deeper we dug, the larger the slabs. It was all very hard on the equipment and the wash plant. Loren and I decided to pause and reexamine our strategy before going deeper and assessing the time involved and the risk to our equipment. Ultimately, we decided to go in one last time and clean what we could off the bottom. We sluiced for eight more hours and recovered thirty-two more ounces of gold! As exciting as it was, we decided to quit while we were ahead. We had to consider the wear and tear on the Cat.

Even so, after finishing the cut and the last cleanup, we recovered eleven hundred troy ounces of gold. It was still early July, and we had taken out nearly as much in June as we had recovered in previous years! We couldn't help but feel Dad had taken care of us and set us up with a good cut, as if he had known he would not be with us the following year. Loren and I considered our situation. We didn't have our former partner to consult, so we decided to reinvest the profits into larger, more efficient equipment to compensate for our manpower loss.

We contacted our friend Walt Neilson, the Cat salesman in Fairbanks, and he had a D8L coming off lease at a landfill project in Yakima, Washington, that would serve us well. The price was right, and we felt it would be a great addition to the operation. We agreed to have it shipped to Alaska when the lease was finished in Yakima. Soon after, Walt came out to the mine to give us the bad news that the D8L was delayed with its contract and would not be available till the following summer. We had been planning on the D8L, and we were very disappointed.

Walt worked with NC Machinery and arranged a D9H they had just rebuilt in Seattle we could rent for $25 an hour for the rest of the 1987 season. NC Machinery went out of their way for us. The normal rent on a 9H was more than $200 an hour. We jumped at the opportunity to bring in the D9H at this price and used it for the rest of the season. We logged 250 hours on it. The machine was massive, and a huge help in moving more material than the D8H.

Mom worked as hard as ever at camp, but we knew how much she missed Dad. We were grateful to Andrea, who often visited and spent time with her. Both women had a solid Christian faith, and Mom comforted Andrea, too, as she was then recently divorced from Stan.

One day Mom was at camp alone, preparing lunch in her trailer.

She looked out the screened door and saw the familiar figure of Joe Vogler striding towards her. As usual, the .44 Magnum revolver was sitting on his hip.

"You tell your menfolk that they're mining on my land," he said to her through the trailer window.

Mom was utterly flabbergasted. She knew we were mining on the ground next to Joe's claims but were within the boundaries. She didn't know quite how to answer other than what she knew.

"I think the boys are on their claim," she said, just to reply.

Her reply wasn't good enough for him. Mom said Joe began what could only be described as a rant about how we were infringing on his land and claim, how we were "foreigners" in Alaska, and how we better move our operation before he had it moved for us. She said she could see his temper rising, and she became more and more afraid of where the scene would end.

Then suddenly, she saw a familiar truck approaching on the gravel driveway. Looking over Joe's head to train her eyes on the newcomer in desperation, Joe continued to berate Mom, her sons, and our entire operation.

The car came to a stop and John Blackwell stepped out. He was a gold buyer for Engelhard, and one of the refiners we worked with at the time. John knew Mom and our family well. He also knew Joe. As he walked up to the trailer, he could hear everything Joe said.

"Hi folks," he said, innocently striding up to the trailer and standing next to Joe. "What's going on today?"

Joe quieted at once. It was as if John's presence snapped Joe out of his rant. He looked from John to Mom and knew he wouldn't get anywhere with John on the scene. He still looked angry and threatening, and John knew he had to defuse the situation.

"Joe, why don't you be on your way? I have some business to discuss with Phyllis," he said calmly.

Joe grumbled something Mom couldn't hear and turned to leave. Mom said she was never so relieved to see someone in her life. When Loren and I heard what happened, we couldn't believe it. It was as if he knew Dad was gone so he could hassle Mom while we were out at the mine. Knowing our neighbor watched every move we made, we were confident we were not on his claims. We had the stakes and map to prove it. How cowardly for Joe to take up his grievance with Mom rather than stopping in at the mine and talking to us! He was tough with a newly widowed woman, but apparently afraid to face us. Joe never set foot in our camp again, nor did we hear from him again about his grievance. He succeeded in terrorizing Mom but would not intimidate us.

*****

In the spring of 1988, Loren flew out to Seattle, and we made a deal on the Cat 245. It was a 140,000-pound excavator with plenty of size for our operation. We shipped both the D8L and the 245 excavator to Fairbanks, and I traveled up to the mine in March to supervise their move to the site for the 1988 season. I contacted Tim McKay and he hauled them up the Steese and into camp without a problem. I returned to Seattle, and Loren and I returned to the mine in early May.

There was a berm of tundra that we had pushed up a previous year. We decided to burn it rather than push it out of the way again. We went to camp and filled two five-gallon cans with a mix of diesel fuel and gasoline. We brought them back to the pile of tundra and poured them onto the brush. The tundra and debris were very damp from the winter, so we felt confident we could have a safe burn to extinguish the pile. We struck a match and stoked enough flames to burn the pile.

We saw the flames flare, and then slowly die out. Thinking the tundra was too wet to burn well, we abandoned the project until later in the summer. Two weeks later, as we were finishing lunch in Mom's trailer, we saw Mom looking over our shoulders out the window.

"Do you have something burning at the Creek?" she asked.

Loren and I spun around and saw a massive plume of black smoke rising from the direction of the tundra pile. We knew immediately our once harmless little fire that we had thought was extinguished had reignited and jumped into the black spruce forest. We jumped up and headed straight for our ATVs and barreled full speed down to the bulldozers. I jumped on the D8L, and Loren followed me with the D8H. We made a few passes to clear the trees and create a firebreak, about one hundred feet wide, to stop the blaze.

We watched the flames lick closer to our firebreak, hungrily seeking their next target to devour. As they hit the firebreak, we watched in satisfaction as the flames stagnated, then slowly began to wane.

Loren and I idled down the Cats, breathed a sigh of relief, and stood talking about how foolish we were to try to burn the brush pile. The fire must have been burning deep in the tundra for two weeks, unbeknown to us. A tiny surviving spark and the environment was enough to resurrect a flame, rip through the brush pile, and skip into the forest. As we stood in shame, we watched the Bureau of Land Management firefighter trucks drive towards us. They jumped out and walked over to us. They couldn't thank us enough for getting the blaze under control. They told us they had seen the smoke and launched two fire bombers out of Fairbanks to extinguish their fire. When they saw we had everything under control, they radioed in a cancellation for assistance.

As they spoke to us, Loren and I were conscious that the discarded cans of fire accelerant were at our feet, but the firefighters either didn't see them or opted not to ask. We accepted their praise and never did admit we were the two firebugs responsible for the fire in the first place. Our guilt was punishment enough. If the fire had gotten away from us, it could have burned its way toward the little town of Central, Arctic Circle Hot Springs, or both. We would never attempt to burn a brush fire at camp again!

With the new Cat 245 in camp, we were excited to start stripping a new cut. Deed and Anna had returned to camp. Linda was home in Redmond, working and waiting to hear something from our adoption agency.

We hired Andrea's brother, Randy, to work with us for the summer. Randy was from Fairbanks and had years of experience in heavy equipment operation and mining. Another miner approached us with a ripper shank to attach to the 245 and help rip through the frozen black muck more easily. He offered us the shank to try, and we set it up on the 245. Once again, we could see the hard pull of the machinery and hear the awful popping sound of the black muck as it stressed the machine's hydraulic system. We blew several hoses on the 245 before we decided to revert to the D8L to perform the ripping.

*****

On May 1, 1988, Andrea came over with a message for us to call Patty Beasley, our case worker with the adoption agency. Linda had just arrived in camp the day before, so I stayed in camp working while Linda went to Andrea's to return Patty's call. Patty told Linda we had been chosen by a birthmother to adopt her baby girl. Although final papers were not signed, we were advised by Patty to work on flights back to Seattle. We immediately packed up and headed to Fairbanks. While waiting for our flight to Seattle, it was confirmed the relinquishment papers had been signed. We had the "go ahead" to head home.

Upon landing in Seattle, we hit the deck running. We had a

crib set up, but needed to shop for the necessities we didn't have, like diapers, bottles, clothes, car seat, stroller, and everything you need for a baby.

The case workers arranged for us to meet the birth mother and birth father in Wenatchee, Washington, on May 6. We loaded the car with the supplies we needed and buckled in the new child car seat. We were leaving home childless; we would return home as parents!

After being introduced to the foster mother of the baby, we met Bill, the birth father. Bill was twenty-one, and very shy and timid. We met Marcia, the birth mother, along with her parents. Marcia was eighteen and just graduating from high school. It was a very emotional time for everyone as Marcia and her parents said their good-bye to Kelsey. We were grateful beyond words to Marcia to entrust her daughter to us. We assured Marcia we would love and give Kelsey the best care possible.

After waiting so long, we finally had a child and our lives had changed forever. We were filled with joy with this new blessing. This experience really hit me when we left Wenatchee and drove over the Cascade Mountains with the empty child car seat. It was now occupied by our sweet, beautiful new daughter.

I stayed in Seattle for a week before leaving Linda and Kelsey behind to get back to work at the mine. Linda stayed home with Kelsey, taking maternity leave to bond with our new addition. Kelsey was a colicky baby, so the first few months were difficult for her, but together they pushed through. After a few weeks, Linda came to the mine with Kelsey and stayed until we shut down in September. My only regret was that Dad never had a chance to meet Kelsey.

At the end of the season, I returned to Seattle and became full-time Mr. Mom whenever Linda was on a trip. Sometimes when Linda was gone, I would visit Mom and help her with things around the house so she could spend time with Kelsey. It was the new normal for our family, and we loved every minute of it.

*****

The 1989 season started with the usual optimism and excitement of the previous seasons. We also felt like celebrities because our family had just been featured in a prominent trade publication called *Timber Producers Magazine*. The publication covered logging activity in Michigan, Minnesota, and Wisconsin. The article told the story of how our family left the wood-producing business to mine gold. It was a nicely written article by Mike Savage, who knew Dad and his history in the pulpwood industry. Since Dad was no longer with us, the article referred to Mom as the "Matriarch of the Clan."

When Deed read this, she was immediately offended. She did not see Mom as a "matriarch" since we were all equal partners in the mine. She also made it clear to Loren that she did not think Mom deserved a third of the mine. However, Loren and I agreed Mom's partnership was nonnegotiable.

As Kelsey grew, Linda and I both thought it best to add an addition onto our Coachman fifth wheel. I bought lumber and supplies to build a 16x20-foot building to extend our living space. Loren and I spent a couple of weeks hammering a lovely building together, but I knew Deed was irritated that Loren was helping me instead of mining. Nevertheless, Linda and I were excited to put in the finishing touches, which meant installing carpeting for the large room. We had ordered the carpet from a supplier in Fairbanks, and since Loren had to pick up Deed from the airport, I asked him to pick it up for me. He agreed and set off for Fairbanks.

While Loren was gone, I worked on the septic system under my fifth wheel. It was a smelly, messy job. I tried not to breathe as I lay under the trailer, removing the awful waste tank. Then I heard Loren's truck drive into camp. Excitedly, I pulled myself from under the trailer, grateful to be in the fresh air and ready to help him unload the new carpet. You can imagine my disappointment when I saw the truck bed was empty as he pulled to a stop.

Deed got out of the truck, Anna in arms. She gave me a curt "hello" and made a beeline for her cabin. I could tell something was wrong, like the couple may have been arguing. I accepted the aborted carpet delivery as collateral damage.

"What's going on, Loren?" I asked.

I could feel his stress and agitation.

"This is my last year," he said. "Deed said it's either mining or her."

He got back into his truck and drove away, leaving me in shock. What I had just heard was harder to stomach and messier and more distasteful to me than the septic system job I just did. I couldn't believe my ears.

Loren and I talked about it two or three times after his initial announcement, but he had made up his mind. Or, should I say, Deed made up his mind for him? She was tired of everything at the mine and the camp, including her in-laws. She was done.

The proclamation made 1989 a long, arduous season of mining. It was as if dark clouds had settled over the camp. We mined the ground on the left limit of Ketchem, closest to our living area. It wasn't the best ground we had, but we were excited to discover the best nuggets of any year on the creek. The largest one was one-half ounce, and most were clean and well worn. It was amazing to think the nuggets had traveled quite a distance down the valley to their final resting place in our cut. Even after so many years of mining gold, most of it fine, it was still a thrill to lay eyes and hands on gold in nugget form.

Loren and Deed set their departure date. I planned to stay later and strip a cut for the following season. One night Loren, Mom, and I gathered and split up our gold for the last time. There were three equal bottles of gold nuggets although one of them had a beautiful one-half ounce nugget. Mom shuffled the bottles around so we could blindly pick, but she didn't do a good job; we knew where the bottle with the best nugget was. Loren quickly snapped up the bottle where the known choice nugget was. Loren packed the nugget bottle with the rest of his season's gold and left. It was another "peace at any price" moment. Mom and I were thankful for the good season and years together on Ketchum Creek.

It was heartbreaking to watch Loren drive away, knowing he would never return. We were like twins, and I felt we were never at our best like we were when we were working together on a project. We had been doing it since we were kids, and it made me sad our mining adventure was over. I also felt angry, especially at Deed. I felt she was a wedge that had been thrust between Loren and me and led our partnership to a bitter end.

Mom stayed with me late that year as I finished stripping the next cut for the 1990 season. When I thought about whether I should return to the mine without Loren, my answer was always yes. I loved mining and the amazing operation we had built. Although I would miss him, I couldn't imagine summer without camp. Luckily, Mom was on board too. Our mining venture, which had been so robust with the four of us (Mom, Dad, Loren, and I), was now down to two. But we would endure.

*****

In the spring of 1990, Mom and I returned to Ketchem Creek. There was still plenty of mining to do there. I found two dependable, experienced guys to help me for the summer, Steve and Vinny Stack.

Vinny was single and lived in Fairbanks, where he raced his sled dogs in many races, including the "Yukon Quest" Whitehorse to Fairbanks. Steve was married and from Fairbanks too. He had a background in placer mining and planned to start his own mining operation near Fairbanks.

After we finished stripping our cut, we proceeded to sluice. The ground was very lean and not paying well. We were doing all we could, but the gold was not there. It was becoming harder to compensate the Stacks.

We decided to suspend our mining on the Fourth of July. However, we had one more payment on the 8L and the 245. Loren had said he wanted to be completely bought out by the end of the season. At the rate we were finding gold, it seemed like an impossible mission. Mom was sixty-five years old now and still determined to keep peace at any price. I was also getting pressure from Linda to end the mining operation, sell what we could, and find work closer to Seattle. Mom voted to suspend the mining operation permanently and I reluctantly agreed. As much as I didn't want to stop mining, it seemed all signs pointed to the end of the era. It was the best decision at the time.

*****

As the news of the closure of our mining operation spread, many people contacted us to buy our equipment. We easily sold cleanup jigs, small pumps, and other light equipment. Stan Gelvin was interested in the wash plant, sluice box, and Cummins pump that fed the wash plant. He asked me to talk with the owners of our claims and offered to buy the equipment if I could convince them to transfer the claims to him. I was successful and arranged for Stan to purchase the equipment. I had started reclamation work, leveling the large dragline tailings piles, but Stan asked me to leave them to indicate what had been mined and what had not. I did as he asked.

I leased a large box truck from U-Haul and loaded my personal things, tools, and some equipment for the return to Washington State. I contacted Tim McKay to come for the D8L, D8H, 175B Michigan loader and 245 Excavator, as well as our 4BT Cummins pump, and take them to his shop in Fairbanks to sell. He hauled the equipment "Tim style," without removing any attachments.

The Stack brothers took our four-thousand-gallon fuel tank for their mining venture they were planning near Fairbanks. Stan offered to buy the Koehring dragline, so we left it on the creek for him. I sold our new building as is, where it was. It was disappointing that Linda and Kelsey did not get much time in it. Loren sold his cabin, and mom sold her trailer to her friends, Wayne and Doris Eames.

As I left the mine, I felt like I was leaving behind a piece of my soul. I loved the freedom-filled life of mining, and I looked ahead to an unknown future. Mining had given Linda and me a nice income. I was able to have the winter months off to spend more time with her and Kelsey and travel together, too. Mining had become my passion, and every year brought new joys and challenges. It was hard to accept that it was over forever.

My brother-in-law, Warren Parker, flew to Fairbanks to make the trip home with me. I picked him up, and we headed down the highway. The shorter route was the ALCAN to Highway 37, and onto the Cassiar Highway through glacier country. We did well on our trip until we had a flat tire on one of the outside duals. Unfortunately, U-Haul did not provide us with a spare tire!

The closest possible place for us to find a tire was in Hyder, Alaska. To get there, we would have to drive out of our way down a risky gravel road with one of the rear dual tires flat. We were very concerned about the heavy load but had no other choice.

We breathed a sigh of relief when we pulled the U-Haul into the tire shop, and they had the tire we needed. The rest of the trip was uneventful, and we would always remember our side trip to the town of Hyder.

Once home, I stored the equipment we delivered by truck in my shop near our home in Redmond, Washington. Loren came out from Wisconsin with his truck and a trailer to pick up the equipment he wanted from the mine. We had a lot of mechanical and air-powered tools to divide among us. In most cases, we had two of everything, including air compressors and welders. We amicably split what we had and loaded his truck and trailer. The mood between us was solemn but friendly. We had both accepted our lives were going to change and we both hoped we would be happy without mining.

It was time to look to the future, no matter how unsure it was. Loren stayed a few days before driving back to Wisconsin. Our next steps were identical; we planned to look for construction work near home.

As he drove away, I wished him well. It was to be a new adventure for us both.

*****

Back in Redmond, I applied for a job with a family-run construction company called Carton and Sons, in Woodinville, Washington, about twenty minutes away. I operated excavators and small finish dozers for them. I also had a Commercial Driver's License (CDL), so I drove dump trucks and hauled my own equipment to different small jobs. The economy in the Seattle area was good, and they had plenty of work to keep me busy. I worked for them for a few months, and they were good to me. As much as I liked the company and the work, losing my independence and freedom after being self-employed for ten years was very difficult for me. After a few months with the company, my entrepreneurial spirit got the best of me. I decided to buy some equipment and go out on my own.

I used my Alaskan gold to buy a nice John Deere 350 dozer and Caterpillar D3 and D4 Dozers. I also found a small dump truck and trailer to move my equipment to and from jobs. I also bought a Caterpillar 426 backhoe/loader, which I knew would help me expand my services. With an ad in the paper and some word of mouth, I could easily pick up work and do more. Initially, I wasn't happy with the amount of work and money I was making, but at least I was independent.

I worked as a small contractor from 1991 to June 1994. Linda was still with the airline, and I was a single dad for two weeks of the month. We had a very safe and loving daycare for Kelsey, but my days were long between working during the day and attending to Kelsey's needs early in the morning and evening.

Most of my work was for small home builders, horse property owners, and some commercial building projects. Scheduling was difficult. Some days, I was needed in two or three places at the same time. Other days, the phone didn't ring. I enjoyed the work and met some good people in Seattle. I also discovered the best people to work for were people with horses needing to improve their pastures with drainage and other improvements. They knew what they wanted and needed, and they willingly paid when the work was complete.

People were good about paying me except on two occasions. One builder of a half-million-dollar home didn't think he had to pay me. The worst offender was a couple who figured I could drag a tree up a hillside and sell it to cover their thousand-dollar invoice. Ironically, they asked me for a second invoice so they could recover half of my fee from another family who would benefit from the work. I thought I would finally get paid after the second invoice but never got a cent.

In hindsight, I would have been better off working for contractors operating their equipment than striking off on my own. It was an expensive experiment in self-employment when I thought my mining days were over. I had no idea that they weren't!

CHAPTER 8

MINING REVISITED

My life went on, hundreds of miles away from my memory of the mine. I was moderately successful with my construction work and a full-time caregiver for Kelsey when Linda was flying. Yet I always kept my eye on the price of gold. And in 1994, I noticed it was climbing.

In Wisconsin, Loren had found work with a construction company in Superior, operating an excavator. We stayed in touch, and I always saw him when I returned to Wisconsin, which I did often, flying on Linda's passes. I would visit Mom, and Kelsey got to know her family better with each visit.

I could tell that Loren was unhappy even before he told me he was. He didn't really enjoy his work. He felt the gnawing, familiar discomfort that any entrepreneur feels when they work for someone else after being on their own. He missed the independence we had and wasn't making the money he did mining gold.

In the spring of 1994, the price of gold hit the level it did when we first started mining—$350 an ounce. The information was like a siren's song for me. I still remembered the long, sunny summer days, the joy of finding gold, and the sights and sounds of being in the wilderness, working side by side with Loren. I thought of it often but had told myself those days were over.

Then one day in June, the phone rang, and it was Loren. We chatted for a while about life and family in general. By this time, Loren and Deed had adopted a little boy from Colombia named

Michael. Anna was nine and Michael was six, just a few months younger than Kelsey. They were doing fine, but once again, Loren mentioned his dissatisfaction at work.

"You know the price of gold is up to $350 an ounce," he said.

"I heard that," I replied. His next words shocked me.

"I think it's time to get back into the mining business," he said.

I was stunned, but excited. There was nothing I wanted to do more than return to mining with Loren.

"Would you look for some mining claims?" Loren asked.

"You bet," I replied, and I was smiling so big I'm sure he heard it.

I couldn't wait to get started! Loren suggested mining ground in the Yukon area of Canada, where the environmental regulations weren't so stringent and the permits easier to get than they were in Alaska. My cousin Doug Green was still living and working in Fairbanks, so I called him first to see if he knew of any open prospects. He was helpful and knew of a guy that had a lead on some ground in Carmacks, Yukon.

As I hung up the phone, my mind swirled with all the plans I needed to make and the possibilities that awaited us. I didn't really think about anything but finding a site. I even forgot to mention anything to Linda, although she figured it out on her own. One day she heard the beep and whirring of the fax machine and went to the office to see a fax coming through. She immediately recognized it as a mining map. She turned to me in surprise and disbelief, realizing my plan. She also knew who was included in the plan.

"Are you sure you want to do this with them again?" she said.

I hadn't really given much thought to the personal side of mining again with Loren and Deed. I recalled how difficult Deed was and how she had made Loren choose between mining and her. I remembered her unhappiness at camp, the way she would poison people with her negative attitude, the teaming against Mom and Linda, the way she would shirk work and keep to herself, and, most of all, her resentment that mining took Loren away from his family. If we started again, nothing would change there. Yet despite everything I knew going in, I had confidence that Loren had cleared this with Deed, and she was onboard. They did everything as a team. I was certain Deed now knew what she was getting into, thought it through, and consented. Either she had grown up or was willing to make the sacrifice for her husband to give him a little more happiness. "It won't be like that again," I said, confident at the time. "It's gonna be different."

I also explained one of the arguments that Loren made to me. He was convinced the price of gold was on its way up. "If we don't get in now, it'll just be harder later," he said. It was optimistic logic, but it certainly made sense to me.

Linda wasn't sold and wasn't very excited about the plan either. We both knew it would be harder this time now that we had Kelsey. However, she went along with it, perhaps adopting my mom's motto about living in a mining community: find peace at any price.

*****

I left for a prospecting trip to Nansen Creek, flying into Whitehorse where I met Deed and Loren. They drove there after leaving the kids with my sister, Brenda. We arrived the same day in Whitehorse, met up at the hotel, and the next morning we drove north for two hours to Carmacks, and followed Mount Nansen Road to the mine.

The road was a slow, fifty-mile drive on a narrow, unpaved mountain road, flanked on both sides by steep slopes. We were the only ones along the lonely stretch of road. As it began to drizzle and the tires on our vehicle started to shift underneath us, we realized how dangerous driving could be.

We finally arrived at Nansen Creek and were greeted by Alfie Gould, the mine watchman. He was older than Loren and I and thought of himself as the mine "Superintendent." He asked how old we were.

"I'm thirty-nine, and Loren is forty-one," I replied, gesturing to Loren.

"Oh, you're just kids" he said, haughtily.

One of his hands only had two fingers, but this handicap didn't stop him from working an excavator well. He thought he had a good deal of mining knowledge, but so did we. Alfie had been staying at the idle mine during the summer to protect the interest of the mine owners, which was a group of four entrepreneurs from Vancouver who also owned the BYG Hard Rock mining property. BYG had opened an operation at Nansen Creek to mine placer gold as they worked on permits and logistics for their hard rock operation. The mine itself had an interesting history.

In 1991, a crew had been hired to prospect the ground, and, in 1992, the BYG group had purchased equipment and hired a crew to mine the lower claims. Poor management and excessive drinking had led to many expensive mistakes. They lost a 966 loader when it tipped over and ended up in a settling pond. Their D9H was backed onto ice and crashed through a deep water-filled test hole. The owners were now looking to sell and recover what they could to reinvest it into the hard rock mine property.

As we surveyed the claims, Loren and I were both confident that we had the knowledge and experience to turn the idle mine into a profitable venture. There was a cut that seemed stripped and ready for sluicing. The wash plant was all set up and ready to go with an enormous trommel, a rotating, drum-like apparatus that would tumble the pay dirt to wash the large and small rocks and screen the finds to five-eighths inch before being sent down the sluice. The trommel barrel was a railroad propane tank that was adapted for mining. It was about 40 feet long made of five-eighths inch thick, T1 steel with six-inch angle iron welded down the barrel for grinding the clay materials into a slurry. The trommel was well built and a very good match for the material that we needed to wash on Nansen Creek.

The mine sale included four pieces of equipment that were already on the property: a 225 Cat excavator, a Cat 980 and 966 wheel loader, and a D9H bulldozer. All of the equipment needed repairs, but we were able to do what needed to be done to get them running well, if the pay was worth it.

We decided the best way to prospect the ground was to take the 225 excavator into the cut that had been stripped. It took longer than expected because the 225 only had one track operating. We limped it around the cut from test hole to test hole. For June, it was a miserable, cold, and windy day, which I estimated was about forty degrees. It reminded me of our mining days on Birch Creek.

Loren and I panned the pay and consistently found twenty-five to thirty colors per pan, which was similar to the values we had seen on Ketchem Creek. The mine was viable!

We spent the night in the camp on Nansen and drove back to Whitehorse the next morning. While driving we discussed the results of our prospecting, and by the time we got to Whitehorse we had talked ourselves out of buying the mine. The location and weather had a lot to do with this decision. It was a very remote location at an elevation of thirty-six hundred feet, which meant colder weather. The road to reach Nansen Creek was treacherous even in sunshine. We reached the hotel and slept on it.

The next morning, things looked brighter to us both. We felt we could overcome the inconveniences of the mine and have a great venture together. We purchased thirty-three claims of good ground, confident the mine was like Ketchem, and we could mine there for a lifetime.

There were also existing buildings at the mine which made it easier to move in. There was bunkhouse trailer, a kitchen, laundry room, and a cook's quarters in the main trailer. We had an extra building we turned into the "gold room" where we could clean the gold in comfort Alfie had staked his claim in the bunkroom in the gold room building.

Loren and Deed drove back to Seattle. and I flew home to Redmond. Linda asked me again if I was sure. She was grudgingly onboard but wasn't as optimistic as I was that Deed would be any different. Despite any nagging misgivings either of us had, we proceeded with the purchase of the claims.

We were on our way to the Fourth of July fireworks when we got the call that our offer had been accepted and we could begin mining on Nansen Creek. We immediately hired an attorney in Whitehorse to help us with the details of the purchase, then spent a busy two weeks packing small equipment, tools, and personal gear to head back to the Yukon. We wanted to get as much work done as possible, even though it was late in the season.

I began preparations right away, with all the optimism that I had that first day we arrived on Birch Creek. I bought a cargo trailer to move my personal things and tools to the Yukon. Loren was bringing up an RV, but my plan was to knock out a wall in the bunkhouse to create a larger living space.

As I packed up the trailer, Kelsey watched me fretfully making trips back and forth to the trailer with my clothes and personal things. Being only six, there was no way for her to understand what was happening. She started crying and as we tried to comfort her, we discovered she thought I was moving out for good! To tell her I was going "to the gold mine" or "gone for the summer" was no comfort. We hugged her closely and assured her everything was fine. We knew that once she saw the mine, it would all be better.

We arrived at Nansen Creek to start work on July 20. It felt surreal to be at a mine again, but our first job, as always, was to get the equipment in shape for the season. Every piece of equipment needed something, and in some cases, more than we expected. The heads on the D9H were cracked and missing, apparently from an overheated engine. The engine needed extensive cleaning and the heads replaced. Both loaders had exposed electrical panels in the cabs that needed attention. The 225 needed repair on the bad track motor and brake replacements.

We made a trip to Whitehorse to get various parts and supplies, including some gold-catching material for the sluice box. We were not able to find the AstroTurf we were used to. Instead, we purchased a "nomad carpet" from a store called Northern Metallic, which was what miners in the area used. When we tried to pay with the first check from our new Canadian Bank account, number 101, the clerk named John raced upstairs to call our bank and check on the available funds. The funds were there, we left with our carpet, and John became a friend of ours who helped us with purchases anytime we were in Whitehorse.

In ten days, we had the equipment running smoothly and we were ready to start sluicing the pay layer. Our equipment was in great shape, but little did we know our crew would be our big challenge this time around!

*****

Alfie was familiar with the mine, so we hired him for our first season. We hired Dave Tochacek, a big, good-looking, strapping guy who was dedicated to his work and became our right-hand man; Jack, a man who was in his fifties and had been in the area mining for some time; and Mike, who was young, single, and around eighteen years old. We were new at hiring in the Yukon, and the Canadian laws were definitely in favor of the employees. We paid well for hourly rates, but at the end of the season, a disgruntled Alfie petitioned the Yukon Government for overtime, and we ended up having to pay it.

Alfie caused lots of problems in his first year with us. He was an alcoholic, and we would see him drag Jack and Mike down a dark road with him. Alfie's wife would drive out on the weekends with a trunk full of Extra Stock Beer for him and his buddies to last the coming week. We didn't quite know how to handle the problem, which was completely new to us. Fortunately, Dave was very responsible and didn't get involved with the nonsense of the other three. His attitude was stellar, and we were glad to have him with us through our first season, as well as many more.

We would wake up in the morning to find empty beer cans strewn around in front of Alfie's bunk room. It was obvious Alfie, Jack, and Mike were having happy hour all night. We asked them nicely to stop casting the cans out the door, but they continued to do it, knowing it bothered us. We were disgusted with their behavior but stuck it out to just get through the mining season and find another more responsible crew for the following year.

The three drinkers caused problems at the mining site too. Alfie was the excavator operator and fed the plant while sluicing. Dave forwarded the pay up to Alfie from the cut. Alfie took great pleasure in loading large rocks into the trommel either out of laziness or just to hear them bang their way down into the barrel. Such large boulders only cause damage to the equipment and should have been set aside. On a couple occasions, Alfie blew a hydraulic hose and ran the excavator until it drained the oil tank. We were convinced that Jack was smoking pot both from his behavior on the job and how inefficiently he pulled the tailings. We walked on eggshells with the crew the entire six weeks we worked together.

At the same time, we had guests who helped release the tension in camp. BYG had sent out a drilling crew and two geologists to diamond drill their hard rock claims. We agreed to house them in return for providing the cook and groceries for the camp. The drilling crew was led by a man named Phil who came with his wife, who became our cook, and their son. They were part of a family operation from the 100 Mile area of British Columbia. They brought their complete crew, equipment, and tools, and were in the field all day and very nice and respectful to everyone. Loren and I were happy to have some more sober people in camp!

One day, Phil shared the sad story of how he lost one of his sons when they drilled near Whistler, British Columbia. He was diamond drilling with his twenty-year-old. Phil left him for twenty minutes to do something and when he returned, he discovered a grizzly bear had trapped his son in the drill shack and killed him. The bear was having his dinner when Phil returned. Phil got his revenge on the bear but still grieved for his son who had been in a truly inescapable position. It was such a devastating event for Phil and his family, and still very fresh in their hearts. You could feel their pain and sadness. It was also a reminder to us how quickly life can change with situations in the bush.

One day, the geologists with the drilling crew bought a leg of lamb to prepare a special dinner as a thank you to all of us in camp. Since they were working in the field, they decided to cook the meat underground like a roast pig to give Phil's wife the night off. They had purchased plenty of meat for everyone and spent a good part of the day tending the fire and cooking the lamb.

The dinner was delicious, and everyone was very appreciative… except Alfie. I'll never forget his unbelievable reply when he was offered a piece of lamb.

"I don't eat no f'n goat," he said.

The cook was planning on serving the remaining leg of lamb for lunch the next day, but Jack had his dog in camp. During the night, Jack raided the refrigerator and fed the leftover lamb to his dog. The cook and the rest of the crew couldn't believe someone in the camp would act so thoughtlessly.

We set up a schedule to give our work crew every other weekend off. It was a chance for Loren and I to collect our thoughts and catch up with maintenance and repairs. The equipment had not been well maintained over the years and the abuse at the hands of our crew didn't help. After working ten to twelve-hour days, the crew was more than ready to leave camp, except for Alfie. Alfie stayed on the creek every weekend and didn't leave once the entire summer. There was always food to eat, and his wife delivered beer every weekend. What more could he want?

While the crew was sluicing, Loren and I were either working on projects in camp maintenance, equipment maintenance, fabricating equipment, or cleaning gold. As usual, we were always trying to improve our operation to make work easier and more efficient. The previous owners had not stripped close enough to the pay dirt, so we stripped off the barren two feet of clean gravel to sluice only the good pay dirt. We replaced our inherited cleanup system with a jig from IRD in Carson City, Nevada. The jig recovered gold quickly from the magnetite black sand and shaved hours off our cleanup time.

We also saw how we could improve the existing trommel and

feed system. We planned to purchase a belt feeder that could feed the wash plant and replace the operator and excavator that we used the first year. The feeder alone would reduce the crew by one man, saving wages and room and board expenses. We could also see the advantage of a steady feed and removing the large boulders, which only hindered gold production.

We finished our first cleanup, and I went into Whitehorse to locate a gold buyer/refiner. We were sure there was one there, but we could not locate the shop. Finally, we connected with two brothers who owned Locksmith Services. They were the contact in Whitehorse that would take our gold, weigh it, and ship it to the Engelhard buyer in Vancouver. We were relieved to finally understand the system and to be working with Engelhard again.

*****

While the Circle mining district in Alaska felt like a tight-knit community, the miners were more independent in the Nansen Creek area. There was a miner named Jack Coglin who mined on Back Creek and later, East Fork. He had been in the sawmill business in British Columbia but had been hard hit with taxes when he sold it. He felt the gold mining business was a way to recover some of his taxes and hold gold for his retirement. Jack was very friendly and the first to come to our camp and introduce himself. We worked with Jack in trading ideas and supplies. We had D9H Cat parts that he could use and a large convex mirror that he needed to feed his sluice box. We had a nice friendship with Jack and his wife, Beryl, and we would visit each other's camps.

Then there was Ted Tullis who mined the claims above us on Nansen Creek with a small trommel that had a track feeder. Ted was an excellent fabricator and built his plant and feeder himself. He had spent a few years on Nansen before we bought the lower claims. I think he regretted not buying the claims we mined because his own were quickly depleted. Ted moved to another creek and the claims were poor. He only mined there a season before closing his business. Bill Tereras mined on Discovery Creek and seldom came down to Nansen. We didn't go up to his claims, and Bill didn't come down to ours. We had a friendly relationship with him but didn't socialize. Bill mined the Discovery claims until 2003 and then moved off to another creek or retired.

In 1994, Ted had a good year and his cook, Glenda, wanted to celebrate with a big party at the end of the season. We were happy to join them, in the same community spirit that we had enjoyed in Alaska. We had arrived as foreigners in Canada but quickly began to feel comfortable and part of the community. However, we immediately sensed an undercurrent of tension among the miners. Jack and Bill seemed to be friends, but Ted was obviously an outsider. We did our best to stay neutral and on good terms with all the miners, and we never learned what happened between them, nor did we ask. Deed and the kids were in camp for most of the summer. I was disappointed to see that she was again, unhappy there. She and Loren had brought along plenty for the kids to do, and they even had a TV, a VCR, and plenty of movies to watch. However, she was the same old dissatisfied Deed that she had been on Ketchem Creek. Any ideas I had about her growing up or being different this time quickly vanished.

Linda brought Kelsey to camp a few times that first summer. The first time, though, she had to call in sick to get the necessary time she needed to make the trip. Kelsey liked camp and it was good for her to see where I was living all summer and why. However, Linda and I both agreed that spending the entire summer at camp would not be beneficial for her. Linda flew back and forth with her for the summer, so each visit was like a mini vacation. As she grew, we arranged for her to attend Bible camps both in Seattle and near our mining camp.

Kelsey played with her cousins a bit, but often she felt like the odd man out. Deed kept the kids close with her, in the trailer most of the time, and we also had different ideas on how to raise our children. Sometimes, her cousins would be watching shows that Linda and I did not think appropriate for Kelsey.

Communication from the mine was somewhat better now. We didn't have to rely on Trapline Chatter. When Linda was away, we could speak by radio phone. It was convenient, but our conversations could be heard by other people in the area with their radio phones dialed into the Carmacks channel. Eavesdropping on people's phone calls was known entertainment in the area. One Friday night, someone we didn't know on the channel was having a discussion with his wife or girlfriend. The girlfriend wanted him to get his a$$ home for the weekend and told him that if he didn't, she would go to the bar and find another man!

The lack of privacy on their phone calls didn't sit well with Linda and the other wives. On one occasion, one of the neighbors listened in on a conversation Deed had with her mother about her mother's health issues. The next time they saw Loren and Deed, they asked how her mother was doing. Deed immediately knew where they had gotten their information and was understandably upset. The following year, we invested in a satellite phone system that cost ninety cents a minute to use. We limited our calls and paid dearly for the privilege of private conversations.

*****

A major difference between Ketchem and Nansen was the wildlife in the area. We rarely saw more than a few squirrels or birds of prey at the other mine. When we first started mining on Nansen, we saw big Woodland Buffalo roaming around on the claims. They looked threatening but were quite gentle. They would peacefully wander wherever they wanted, including our camp. One day, Deed was on the back deck of the laundry and kitchen building, hanging clothes on the laundry line behind the building when she was surprised by a buffalo walking just past her on the deck. I can only imagine she froze up against the wall and let the animal pass.

At the mine, we saw the buffalo use our equipment to scratch their backs, and they grazed nearby, ignoring us. We shared the creek with these docile giants for several years. Then they moved deeper into the hills. Our friend Bruce Wheeler and his wife Grace would hunt them in the fall for subsistence. Bruce and I were friends the entire time we mined on Nansen. He helped us on many occasions, and we helped him too. Occasionally, in appreciation, he would give us buffalo meat that we would cook into a tasty stew.

I was never a hunter, but Loren had hunted back in Wisconsin. There were plenty of game in the area, including moose. One evening, Bruce pulled up to our camp in his Polaris ATV with a quartered moose. Some friends of his had been hunting moose and via satellite phone, asked Bruce to come and pick up their first moose so they could stay out and hunt another. He consented, even though he had been drinking whiskey. Now he needed our help unloading the moose from his Polaris ATV to a truck parked at the BYG camp.

Bruce had the hind quarters in the back of his ATV and the other half on his trailer. We drove ahead to the BYG camp and were waiting for Bruce. When he didn't arrive, we went back to look for him on the road. The hitch on the trailer had broken and half the moose was under the upside-down trailer in the ditch. Bruce was standing there, trying to decide what to do.

Together, we tipped the trailer over and loaded the moose

quarters into Loren's truck. We followed Bruce back to the BYG camp. While Loren and I transferred the two front quarters into the friend's truck, Bruce grabbed a hind quarter from the back of his ATV. Wanting to show us how strong he was, he grabbed the quarter off the ATV with a mighty heave. He immediately pitched forward from the weight before he swung backwards, overcompensating, until he completely lost his balance and landed flat on his back with the moose quarter on his chest unable to get up. I'd say the moose got his revenge!

Bruce was in tune with the wildlife, though, and couldn't stand to see them suffer or wasted. One night, Loren and I saw a caribou limping along on three legs, obviously shot and suffering. When we told Bruce, he immediately knew who was hunting in the area, and was very concerned for the caribou. He was worried it would fall victim to a hungry wolf pack and die a very difficult and painful death. He wanted to find it, give it a quick and painless death and either use the meat himself or find someone that needed it. He picked up his rifle and immediately left us.

Woodland caribou were everywhere in the Nansen Valley during the summer months. They are larger and darker in color than the lighter-colored, barren-ground caribou typically seen in Canada. The bulls with their massive, sprawling, arched antlers were always an impressive sight. The herds were unaffected by our presence, and many days, they would spend the entire day nearby and visible to us.

One day I was working on stripping a cut near the confluence of

Discovery Creek. As I was backing the Cat up and looking over my shoulder, I was startled by a large caribou bull standing on the edge of the wall watching me. The caribou are very curious and docile. Loren and I were working on some of our equipment one day and a group of young, female caribou came within thirty feet of us, just mulling around. They had been watching us for several weeks and had gotten brave enough to come close. The sounds from the equipment didn't seem to bother them at all, and we even caught them peeking around the equipment, curiously. They spent hours walking along our mined areas and on our old settling ponds, perhaps preferring our safe, open area to the mosquito-infested tundra.

On August 1, we would hear the first gunshots of the caribou hunting season. The caribou would disappear up into the hills, and we wouldn't see them until the next summer. The valley was not a safe place for them once the hunting started, and they knew it.

Loren and I felt an attachment to the caribou that spent their summers in the valley with us. We wanted to do what we could to protect our buddies. We asked Deed to make us a "No Hunting" sign, and we erected a roadblock and placed the sign on it. The roadblock stopped vehicles from driving in and hunting on our claims. It also kept us safe from stray bullets.

One afternoon, Loren and I were having a cup of coffee, sitting between our service truck and a piece of equipment, when we heard thundering hooves pounding the gravel and coming right at us. Before we could stand up, we saw a caribou cow and her young calf running right past us. We stood up and walked where we could see them as they ran downstream. Right behind them was a timber wolf, hot on their tracks. As wolves often traveled in packs, we wondered if there would be one or more wolves waiting for these tired animals downstream. Witnessing the circle of life by watching a predator pursue their dinner is truly memorable.

*****

After finishing the sluicing season, Loren and I let the crew go and closed the camp. Alfie expressed his desire to stay as summer caretaker, but we took the opportunity to tell him he would not be returning the next year because of his drinking and behavior. He was immediately enraged, feeling he had the right to stay, but we held firm.

Alfie left camp before we did but we know he returned after we left. The next year, we opened the camp to find missing supplies, rotting food in the refrigerator, and dirty dishes in the sink. We were thankful we had made the decision not to hire him back.

Despite our labor problems, it had been a good year that proved Nansen could be a profitable mine for us. Deed had survived the season, and she and Loren were planning to come back in 1995. We were on a roll!

CHAPTER 9

IN THE SWING

Working in the Yukon, it's always important to be aware of your surroundings. Dave was the first one of our crew to spot a grizzly. The bear was eating blueberries up on the slope above our cut and utterly unconcerned with us and the noise we made on the valley floor.

Another time, Loren and I were in the shipping container where we kept the gold cleaning jig. We heard something outside, and walking right past the shipping container about one hundred feet away was a large grizzly bear. We looked at each other, realizing he could have trapped us had he been curious enough to walk into the shipping container. We may have met the same fate as Phil's son. Besides wildlife, there were many other threats to the stability of our venture in 1995, including troublesome employees, equipment woes, and family dysfunction.

Before we headed up for the season, Loren had located a suitable belt feeder at FabTec in Moscow, Idaho. I took an inspection trip and asked for some modifications in the build. They denied my requests and informed me I would have to make the changes myself. I was disappointed, anticipating the inefficiency of redoing their work. However, I arranged the transport of the feeder by truck to Seattle and then onto the barge to Skagway, Alaska. A truck would haul it the additional six hours to Nansen Creek.

When the belt feeder arrived, we made the necessary changes

to fit into our trommel. We removed the grizzly bars and turned it around to discharge boulders to the other side. The trommel barrel was a railroad propane tank, adapted for mining. It was seven feet in diameter and forty feet in length. It was massive and hard to move but very efficient in washing boulders and creating a slurry before sluicing. We cut the end of the trommel open to insert the feeder inside the barrel, which itself was made of five-eighths-inch wide T1 steel with six-inch angle irons welded down the length of the barrel for breaking down the clay material.

The feeder was a very good match for our needs, but it was so efficient that during a test run, we discovered we needed to slow it down. The trommel could not wash material fast enough to keep up with the feeder! First, we tried changing the existing 440 three-phase motor to a slower one, but the feeder was still too fast. Next, we tried to weigh down the swinging gate that admitted the slurry to the belt. It helped, but we needed to slow it even more. Finally, we changed the sprocket on the chain drive, which resulted in a workable feed rate of one hundred yards per hour. We were ready to feed the cut.

We had a much better crew for 1995. We declared that we would have a "dry" camp to prohibit anyone with a drinking problem. Dave returned, and we had a new man, John Pransic. John was temperamental and moody but had worked reliably for Ted Tulles for years. We set him working on the tailings end of the sluice box while Dave fed the pay dirt into the new belt feeder. Loren dug the drainage with the 225. I would stack pay for Dave to haul to the new feeder. Dave was conscious of keeping the sluices running steady and became a talented loader operator. We could always count on him; he seemed to have our best interests in mind. On the other hand, John was more unpredictable, and sometimes his moods made us uneasy.

One day, John retired to his room to clean his gun. He seemed to be sitting in his room for quite some time, all alone. As he was often unpredictable, everyone in the camp was on edge. When he finally emerged from his room, unarmed, he was completely ignorant of the stir he had caused in the camp. Nothing happened, but John was not the easiest employee to have around.

As the season wore on, we knew the tires on both loaders needed replacing. We finally had a major tire failure on the 980, and, of course, it happened on a weekend. We parked the 980 and used the 966 to feed and take tailings just to stay in production. To make matters worse, the tire on our 966 then failed, but, luckily, Jack Coglin had one for us in his spare pile. We changed the tire and were back in business.

John volunteered to operate the 966, feeding and pulling tailings. Over dinner, he told us that he had tried to destroy the tire we just put on so he could get some time off. He said it as a joke, but Loren and I were not laughing. We knew there was truth in what he said, and it was not funny to us. The only time you're making money in a placer mine is when the sluice is running, and John operated the equipment to make that happen. In hindsight, such an admission perhaps should have been cause for dismissal, but at that point, letting him go was more trouble than it was worth.

Loren and I eventually bought a new set of tires for both loaders. After a few years, tires can be a struggle to remove without the proper tools, so we traded an ounce of gold with a fellow at the hard rock mine for a tool that we could use with our "Hydraulic Porta Power" to break the beads off the rims. We became very good at changing tires!

*****

Phil's wife had done a great job of cooking for us in 1994, but we needed to find someone new for 1995. Loren and I were in Carmacks on the Friday before the crew was set to arrive on Monday. We still needed a cook and were desperate. We stopped in at the Gold Panner Restaurant and met Rose, our waitress. Rose was a heavy-set woman about our age from Quebec City, Quebec. While having our dinner, we told Rose of our search for a cook, and she immediately offered to come out the following week and fill the position. Loren and I looked at each other, assuming she must cook if she worked in a restaurant. We left Carmacks, relieved that we had scored in the "cook department."

Dave was arriving at the mine the following Monday, so we asked him to pick up Rose. He brought his fishing gear with him, and Rose told him she was interested in fishing too. She had packed her Zebco 202 spinning reel mounted on a fishing pole, rubber boots, and the excitement to fish. Rose had already taken an interest in Dave and thought she had found a fishing partner, but she didn't realize Dave was married and uninterested in fishing with her. After a long day's work, Dave slipped out of camp and fished alone.

The next morning, Rose prepared her first meal for us. With new cooks, we are a patient group with low expectations for fancy meals, especially early in the season. However, Rose pushed us to our limits. She did fine on the first breakfast. Then, Rose saw the picture of spaghetti on a can of tomato sauce and figured it was a recipe. She cooked pasta, opened a can of tomato sauce, poured it on the noodles and called it lunch. It neither looked nor tasted good, but we choked it down anyway. As I said, we were patient with the new cooks.

Rose often joined us in conversation, corralling her large frontside into position at the end of the table. One day, John, the only single guy at camp, told us about a girl he had dated over the weekend.

"She was a bad girl too," he said, suggestively.

Rose's eyebrows shot up, and she looked around the table. "I can be a bad girl, too," she announced.

For a moment, you could hear a pin drop, and some of our forks stopped mid-air. The four of us stared at the table and didn't dare look up. We knew what she meant, and nobody was interested.

We toughed out the first few days on Rose's sorry cooking, and on Thursday, I had to make a trip to Whitehorse for more supplies. I asked Rose for a grocery list. She included several bottles of wine and spirits alongside thc other staples we needed. She said she needed them for cooking, but Loren and I suspected it was for her consumption. I left for Whitehorse with no intention of filling her liquor order.

The next day, I returned to a very disgruntled crew. We had purchased six boxes of Kraft Macaroni and Cheese Dinner for our kids when they were in camp. While I was away, Rosanne cooked all six boxes at once and then served the macaroni to the crew for both lunch and dinner the next day. I was about to be served from the same pot for lunch myself.

Loren and I sat down with her, and Rose realized she had to redeem herself.

"I'll fix you a good dinner tonight," she said. Without hesitation, Loren spoke up.

"No, you won't," he replied, "because you won't be here tonight." Enough was enough. Loren told Rosanne she had an hour to pack her bags, and he would take her back to Carmacks and the bus stop. Rose retired to her room and tore up everything she could, destroying a woven basket and her pillow. She left her new fishing boots and her fishing pole in shambles on the floor. In an hour, she was driving out of camp with Loren. He said she begged him to turn around and promised to do a better job if he would give her a second chance, but Loren just kept driving.

After Loren returned, the four of us went to the kitchen to scratch up some dinner. Dave told us when he originally brought Rose out from Carmacks, she had blown her nose in her hand and rubbed it on her jeans. Almost in unison, we asked Dave why he hadn't told us this before!

The Yukon Employment Office in Whitehorse then sent us Linda R. Linda had cooked at the Frazier Border Crossing and was a professional cook by trade. She came in uniform with a good attitude and was an excellent match for our needs. She was a loud and proud lesbian with many other skills besides cooking. She would sweep the floors after meals and pan gold from the sweepings that fell off our shoes as we ate. After completing her work, she would strap on her tool belt and scrounge around the camp for lumber and plywood. She built a nice canopy for her pickup truck bed to protect her cargo. We were all surprised at how skilled and hardworking she was. Linda stayed with us till the end of the season and was excellent at helping us close up the kitchen and camp. In short, 1995 was the season we got the bugs out of our equipment and became genuinely productive. We were all set to return in 1996. And return, we would!

*****

In the spring of 1996, we decided to address the Cat 980C loader. It was leaking oil into the coolant, which was a sign of problems in the cylinders and head. We made arrangements with the BYG hard rock mine owners to use their shop to do some engine rebuilding. We pulled the head and oil pan down, rolled new bearings in the rods, and installed new pistons and liners. We installed a nine-inch Oberg oil filter to monitor the oil and expose any contaminants after the rebuild. We were pleased with the work and thankful BYG had allowed us to work inside and undercover in their shop.

We also decided to head off in search of a new cook. Linda and I drove to Kelowna, British Columbia, to talk with Gail and Carl. Gail was a good friend of Jack and Beryl Coglin. We were treated to dinner at Gail's home and found her to be an excellent cook. We invited both of them to come and work with us that summer. Carl wanted to help as much as possible but had failing health because of cedar lung disease. He had previously worked for Jack as a millwright in Jack's Kelowna area sawmill.

Gail and Carl drove their motorhome to live at the mine for the summer, and Loren and I helped them set up a septic system. Somehow, they never left the mine. Even on weekends, when Loren and I looked forward to taking a break, they were always underfoot. Loren and I needed the time away from the crew to recharge and catch up on maintenance and repairs. Finally, we plainly asked them to take a weekend off. They drove away in the motorhome but returned two days later, after getting a flat tire. Gail was unreasonably angry about what had happened. It was then we learned she had decided to stop taking her antidepressants while in our camp, and the incident had set off her problems. Soon after, they left camp, and the hunt for a new cook was on.

Loren and Deed hired Tina from the Government Employment Office in Whitehorse. She was a competent cook in her late twenties and came to camp with her two-year-old son, which created liability and safety concerns. For example, Loren and Deed had a miniature Pomeranian named Cody. One day Tina's son threw the little dog off the kitchen deck and broke the dog's leg! It was very upsetting for everyone in camp. Cody was a little dog but filled with might and spunk… usually.

One day a grizzly wandered into the camp and the little dog alarmed the bear with his little yips. Before anyone could stop him, Cody charged the bear and ended up chasing it out of camp! We were surprised that the bear didn't make a meal out of Cody, but either he wasn't hungry, didn't feel there was enough to make much of a meal, or he just didn't want to be bothered. Either way, Cody saved the day. Yet another time, we had a lynx stop for a visit in camp. Cody hid under one of the buildings until Deed chased the lynx out of camp. Once again, it could have been the end of little Cody.

Loren and I were well aware of the dangers of luring bears to camp and were very careful with garbage, one of their greatest attractions. We hauled our garbage to the Carmacks dump on a regular basis. When we left camp in the fall, we were always concerned a bear would break into the kitchen while we were gone. Luckily, it never happened.

However, just like a meddlesome bear, Tina was the person in our camp causing a lot of trouble. If more than two women in camp was a problem, Tina was the third that proved the saying correct. She liked to stir things up and made up lies to succeed. She was friends with Deed, and they would often team up against Linda. Tina was there the only time Mom came to visit us in the Yukon. Mom was enjoying retirement from mining and spending time with her grandchildren. However, she had fond memories of her mining days and even missed it.

"Oh, how I wish I could be with you to help," she had said to us, several times. There was still a part of her that longed for the mining life, working with us, and cleaning the gold.

I suggested to Linda that we take a few days off and take Mom to Dawson City. It was a beautiful five-hour drive away and an interesting town to visit with a rich history from the gold rush days. When Tina overheard us talking, she told Deed. Deed immediately made reservations for her family and Mom at a Dawson hotel.

The crew was also unhappy about her lies and scheming. After a while, I knew something had to be done, so I decided to fire her at my first opportunity. Loren and Deed were about to make the weekly supply trip to Whitehorse, so I decided to end Tina's employment the same day they left. Tina knew what was coming, so she arranged for transportation to Whitehorse that morning and quit before I could fire her. She trashed the cook's quarters as she packed and left her son's dirty diapers in the room for Linda to clean up.

Loren was angry and blamed Linda and me for Tina quitting.

"Now I have to find another cook in Whitehorse," he complained. However, there was no attempt made during his two days in Whitehorse. Linda was left to do the cooking (as punishment) for the next week until we could travel to Whitehorse ourselves to hire another cook.

Linda and I went to the Government Employment office and found Aggie. Aggie was an intimidating Austrian with the personality of a pit bull. However, she was an expert at selling herself and made so many promises we would have felt foolish if we had not hired her. We let her know we had three kids in camp, and of course, Aggie told us she was "great with kids." It didn't take long to realize that Aggie wanted nothing to do with the kids in camp.

She had also embellished her cooking skills. One morning I choked down the half-cooked eggs she served and lost them on the trail to the mining cut. Loren was behind me on his four-wheeler and almost lost his own breakfast as he watched mine hit the dirt. It is interesting how people claim to be cooks but cannot fry an egg.

While we were sluicing, Loren and I would eat an hour earlier than the guys running the plant. After we ate, they would go up to the kitchen for lunch, and Loren and I would either run the plant or do a cleanup. One day, Loren and I went up to eat lunch, which was greasy chicken Aggie was serving for the third time. It wasn't worth eating, and of course, we complained to the cook.

"Next time I'll skin the f#*king chicken," she snarled.

We returned to the mine and gave the guys their lunch break. When they returned, we asked them how they liked the greasy chicken.

"Huh?" they replied. "We had roast beef and mashed potatoes and gravy."

Either Aggie took our critique to heart, or she just had it in for us.

During the blueberry and low bush cranberry season, Aggie would spend a lot of time picking berries when she wasn't preparing meals. We were okay with her picking berries, but hoped she would make a few blueberry pancakes or muffins for us. We never saw any berries. She packed them all up to take them home with her.

Once again, a drilling crew from BYG stayed with us for a few weeks in 1996 as they drilled placer mining ground in the area. We agreed to feed and house them for $50 per day, per person. Aggie wasn't happy as we had now added three more workers in camp and at the table. One morning, the drilling crew was in the kitchen with us, and Aggie asked a young driller what he wanted on his sandwich for lunch. The young fellow hesitated for an instant, and Aggie snapped at him.

"When I ask you a question, answer me," she fumed.

Aggie's attitude was so rude and cranky to the drilling crew that we had a meeting with them. Together, we decided to let her go and share the cooking duties between us. We finished the season without her and with substantially better cooking among the rest of us. It had been a good, solid year. With the exception of our cooks, our crew was in a good rhythm and finished the season strong.

*****

1997 was the year we found a drift shaft in our cut. Drifting is hand mining used in the early 1900s. The drift shaft was a large hole, delving deep into the earth and supported by cribbing built from black spruce cut into three or four-foot lengths to give the mine structure. We could see some of the steam pipes the miners had used to pump warm air down to thaw the muck and gravel to gain access to the gold-bearing diamicton clay. Over the years, the vertical shaft filled with water and froze, and the walls would form an amazing crystal cave to be explored. As we stripped away the earth around the shaft with our mighty machines, we realized how much easier it was to mine in the present day. By the time we hit the pay layer, we had uncovered the shaft to reveal a hollow, twenty-foot high, square tower. Even unearthed, the shaft continued eighty feet underground, and was part of the land's history for more than one hundred years.

We left the structure in place to mark the location of the drift for posterity's sake. In total, we found three such shafts below Discovery Creek on Nansen. In one shaft, the miners had dug too deep and stopped in boulder clay, where there was no gold. I'm sure they were very disappointed to have done all that work for nothing. At the confluence of Discovery Creek, they dug a lateral tunnel about eighty feet long, which I'm sure didn't pay well either.

Deed continued to outwardly show her discontent at camp, and her unconcern for anyone in camp except Loren and her children. Since she did her own cooking for her family's dinners, she kept fresh produce at her trailer. When the fresh fruits and vegetables arrived from Whitehorse, Deed would donate her week-old supply to the camp kitchen and restock her personal supply with the freshly arrived ones.

Deed kept Loren to herself as much as possible. When it was my week to go into Whitehorse, I would often return to camp and hear how Deed had monopolized Loren's time during working hours. "It sure is good to have you back," they would tell me. "When you're away, Loren spends most of his time in camp."

Deed was a talented hairdresser and would cut Loren's hair on the days I was gone. The haircut would keep him away from the mine for hours. Upon my return, I could easily tell what had been done or not done even before the crew told me.

One day when I needed a haircut, I asked Deed for a trim. I sat down in the chair for her but did so hesitantly. Tension had been high in the camp for a few days, and I knew Deed was unhappy with me. I never dreamed she would let her negative feelings about me affect her professionalism, but it was my worst haircut ever. My next trip to Whitehorse included a stop at the "Main Event Salon" to get my hair shaped up. I never requested a haircut from Deed again.

One week, Linda came to visit with Kelsey and brought with her a workbook on communication that she had received from a friend who was a management expert. Linda and I met with Loren and Deed, expecting to work through some exercises and clear the air. Our goal was to get to a place where everyone felt heard, and we could openly discuss and resolve our disagreements. We talked about using "I" language between us. "I" language is when you tell someone how you feel rather than accusing them of making you feel that way. In other words, saying, "I feel unappreciated when the camp is a mess," rather than saying, "You never clean up after yourself."

Linda posed a question to us as a group.

"How should we tell others when something is bothering us?"

"I think scream, holler, and yell," laughed Deed.

Soon after, we ended the meeting as it seemed to be going nowhere.

"Maybe I should go and let you take over here," I said wearily to Loren.

"Oh no!" Loren replied. "I'm not doing this without you!"

Even as we failed to talk things through with Deed, at least Loren and I could talk through our issues. After we had been running the sluice boxes for three or four hours, we would dismiss the other guys and spend time loosening up the riffles together, each taking a box to work on. It was our time to discuss matters of importance, like the operation, the employees, our wives, the kids, etc. The discussions weren't always friendly. Some of them escalated, especially when I mentioned Deed's behavior. Loren didn't want to hear about it. However, the next day we were back at the mine, working peacefully side by side.

Our crew in 1997 consisted of Dave Gravett and Brad Katanko. Dave had been a truck driver hauling concentrates from a mine in Faro to the barges in Skagway. When the mill closed, Dave was happy to find work with us. Brad had worked with us the previous year. He brought his friend, Bill, to serve as our cook. Bill had plenty of stories to tell, but not an explanation why his Canadian social insurance number did not match his name. He was collecting disability although he looked fine. Our accountant, Thelma, warned us not to become an accomplice to any kind of scandal. Bill had to go.

The search for a cook was on again. Sharon arrived with her husband, who worked with us on the equipment. We didn't like that Sharon walked around the kitchen in nylon stockings, but her cooking was okay. It was her attitude that needed work. One day, Sharon served potato salad for lunch. Dave grabbed a bottle of ketchup bottle and glopped it on top, right in front of her. She went into hysterics, asking repeatedly why anyone would mix ketchup into her signature dish. Another time Brad walked through a door closer to the kitchen than the dining area and Sharon jumped all over him for using the wrong door. We had to let Sharon go. Her attitude quickly became a liability.

We hired our third cook for the season, Irya, a young Swedish woman in her late twenties who came to us through the Government Employment office. Irya was quiet and did her work as expected. She spent some of her nights visiting someone at the BYG mine. She was always back in camp to have breakfast ready for the crew. Irya got along best with Dave, and they would explore the area during the evenings.

One morning I went down with the crew to get the plant

running and had to make a quick trip back to camp to get something I had forgotten. I was on the deck when Irya came out of the shower room with a towel on her head and a minimum of clothing. She walked past me like I wasn't there and was unfazed by my surprise return to camp. I was embarrassed but apparently, she wasn't. Irya finished the year with us and helped Loren and I close camp.

Irya didn't return in 1998, so we had Lin Quaedvleg cook for us the entire summer. Lin was the best cook we had at the mine. Her meals were always healthy, she made good use of the groceries, and never wasted food. She was great with the kids and even spent time doing art projects with them. I built a fire pit, and Lin would come up to our place in the camp to make smores and spend evenings visiting. Lin was a hard worker, and we appreciated her effort and attitude, especially after having some difficult cooks in camp. We were hoping we could get her to return in 1999, and she did.

Lin loved to cook soup and her soup was always delicious. However, one day early in 1999 after her return, I made the horrible mistake of expressing my displeasure at being served soup too often. After seeing soup once again on the table in front of me, I foolishly made the comment, "Soup, soup, soup!" in a somewhat frustrated tone. Unfortunately, Lin overheard, and if it wasn't for my wife's friendship and diplomacy with her, we would have been without a cook early in the season. I was reminded of my statement often and lived to regret ever making the remark!

*****

In 1999, BYG shut down from financial mismanagement. They had many creditors, including Loren and me. BYG had high-graded the gold reserves and built up their stock value. When the reserves were depleted, the original four investors sold their shares. They were well aware the good ground was gone, and gold production would plummet. They bailed out just before the stock valued at $1.30 or so dropped to three cents a share. Their cyanide-laden settling pond was leaching through the dam and the contaminated water had to be pumped back into the pond.

Our friend Bruce Wheeler was hired to stay onsite to maintain the pumps twenty-four hours a day, seven days a week to prevent the leakage from killing the fish. We were told if the dam broke, it would kill every fish from Carmacks to the Alaska border in the Yukon River. The Canadian Federal Government was left with the expense of cleaning up BYG'S environmental disaster. Unfortunately, independent miners are notorious for taking the money of small investors and leaving them penniless. To run a mine efficiently over the long term, miners must take poor paying reserves along with good paying reserves and build a sustainable average over time. The BYG scam hurt many investors, workers, and businesses who supported them in Whitehorse. Fortunately, we were only out $1,500—far less than many people we knew.

During the two years the hard rock mine was in operation, the road between Carmacks and the BYG mine became quite dangerous, especially during Friday night shift change. The crew leaving for the weekend would already be drinking when they left the mine, and they raced to see who could make the best time to Carmacks. The Yukon Government Road crews had improved conditions by clearing the ditches and corners of brush and grading the road. Unfortunately, this only increased everyone's travel speed and made Mt. Nansen Road even more dangerous.

One day when BYG was still in operation, Deed was scheduled to fly into Whitehorse to join Loren, Linda, and me at camp. We were in the room when Loren got a call from Deed that she had a layover in Vancouver. She was unhappy because her makeup was coming on a later flight.

"I'm just going to just put a bag on my head," she remarked. Loren, Linda, and I couldn't help but laugh, but Deed didn't appreciate us laughing at her pain. She emailed Loren that she hoped he would drive into the ditch on his way to pick her up the next day.

Loren set out on a Friday, the most dangerous day on Mt. Nansen Road, to pick up Deed. When they were heading back to camp, two vehicles turned a corner at very high speed, far out of their lane and heading straight for Loren. He had no choice but to swerve into the ditch. The next day we learned that a worker was killed that night when his vehicle left the road. They found him in the creek, under his truck. Perhaps the moral of the story is not to curse people, for it may land on you!

We had a neighbor named Bob Marshan. His partner's name was Marlene, and they were a little older than us and very friendly.

They even invited us to dinner a few times when we were between cooks. Marlene was a sweetheart; Bob was a drinker.

Bob had sold his claims on Dolly Creek, but he kept an eye on the new owners. Bob knew that the government required claim owners to make "assessments," or "improvements" on their land and to report them to the Mining Recorder in Whitehorse. If claim owners failed to do the required work and report it, the claim could be forfeited and re-staked. Fortunately, our claims were covered for forty years and in good standing. However, in 1999, Bob turned the owners of his former claim into the Mining Recorder for fraudulent assessment reporting and re-staked the mining claims for himself. He was finally going to mine his claims.

Bob and Marlene had little mining experience. One day, when we were working on our equipment in the spring, Bob pulled up to us and climbed out of a fancy one-ton truck with a new welder, fuel tank, and tools. He enjoyed showing off his new ride and telling us about his mining plans while Marlene crawled under the Cat D9 on her hands and knees to see what we were up to. I was impressed with her curiosity and desire to learn.

Bob told us he had made a deal with a lawyer to "grubstake" him, so he had a rumored $200,000 to work with. He had found a nice little trommel wash plant from Barkerville, British Columbia, and moved it up to the creek. He also had rented a Cat 966D and Hitachi Excavator from Whitehorse and hired Larry Tricker from Carmacks to do some stripping for him with his D8H dozer. His plant was nicely fabricated and was a nice size and fit for Dolly Creek. However, as problems arose with the equipment, Bob quickly discovered he was in over his head.

One day the rented 966 loader had a flat tire. Bob was ranting and raving that it was up to the owner of the loader to come out and fix or replace the tire when we all knew that was not how renting worked. Another afternoon, Loren was in Whitehorse when a heavy rainstorm hit. Bob came down and asked us if we could help him save his pond. We knew if his pond dam broke, it could take out our camp generator, so I sent two of our operators to get the loaders running and bring up some oversized rocks from our plant to fortify the spillway on Bob's pond. We hauled the rocks steadily for a couple hours, and I was operating the D8H Cat, trying to maintain a cascade for the water to flow and not cut and drain the settling pond. Bob was hauling gravel but had obviously been drinking because he was dumping the gravel onto the slope, causing more harm than good. After a couple hours, we finally had the water under control, and the pond was no longer a danger to our generator.

The season didn't go well for Bob and Marlene. Alcohol and a poor yield of gold got the best of Bob, and he left the creek in an angry outburst, leaving Marlene behind to finish the last cleanup. Marlene closed up camp and took care of all the work and headaches he left behind. We helped her do the last cleanup. As I ran the concentrates across the jig, I noticed a nice half-ounce gold nugget dancing down the screen. I quickly picked it up and handed it to

Marlene. It was the highlight of her summer, but I was shocked when she decided to give it to Bob after the way he had treated her.

When we returned to Nansen the next spring, Bob's equipment was gone. The lawyer had sent trucks to pick up anything that could be sold to recoup investment money. It was the end of Bob's mine on Dolly Creek, and an example of the many fly-by-night mining attempts that we saw during our years in the Yukon.

Now four years into our venture, we had a rock-solid operation. As we looked to the millennium though, we were at one with the world, expecting something extraordinary to occur to mark Y2K. I hoped for us it would not be a departure of Deed from our camp. She grew more discontented with every passing day, and I did not want to lose Loren.

CHAPTER 10

SURPRISES & SETBACKS

When the clock struck midnight on January 1, 2000, to begin the new millennium, the world didn't end. Neither did our desire to get back to mining in the summer. 1999 had been a good year for us, and we had set aside five hundred troy ounces with Golden West, the refiner we were using at the time. Linda and I had planned to spend the millennial celebration with my brother and his wife on the Oregon Coast. On our way down to Lowell and Barb's on Interstate 5, I spotted a Cat 988 loader for sale just off the highway. Suddenly, I had a vision of this machine on our mining claims. The potential was exciting.

"Hey, on the way home I think we should take a look at that monster," I suggested to Linda.

"Only if we can stop at the outlet stores too," she bargained.

The deal was struck. So, on the way back to Washington, we pulled over to the side of the road by the loader and I climbed through a fence to take a closer look. The machine looked good, and we journeyed on to the outlet stores to complete the agreement.

Loren and I decided to buy the loader, debating whether we should sell our gold and pay cash or set up a loan. We ultimately decided to sell three hundred ounces of our five hundred troy ounces of gold. We purchased the loader in cash, taking what was left as a personal draw.

On February 1, 2000, I was working on the bookkeeping when

I received a call from my friend, Garry Hutchison, a parts guy at Finning in Whitehorse. "I hope you didn't have any gold with Golden West," Garry said. "They just filed chapter eleven."

My heart sank as we still had two hundred ounces of gold on account with them. At the same time, I was thankful we paid for the 988 in cash! We were not the only miners affected by this unfortunate loss. Our tax accountant in Salmon Arm, British Columbia, had several placer miners involved and asked if we would be a part of a class action suit to recover our gold. Through their efforts, we recovered fifty percent of the gold we lost in two years.

*****

Looking ahead to the 2000 season, we hired Dennis and June from Nanaimo, Vancouver Island, to help us. Dennis did the cooking, and June came along with him. Dennis was a good cook and kept the crew happy. He hoped to start a business selling pot pies and experimented on us to get the recipe right. Dennis said the amount of liquid in the pie was the most critical piece of the recipe, so he served us pies of various densities. Luckily, all his pot pies were delicious and kept us satisfied throughout the summer.

However, we did have an issue at breakfast. Dennis was inconsistent with his eggs. Some days, they were runny and raw; others, overcooked and rubbery. Both Loren and I were very particular about our eggs. It all came to a head one morning when Dennis set a plate of undercooked eggs in front of Loren. He took one look at them and stood up.

"I'm going to teach you how to fry an egg," he said to Dennis, heading for the kitchen.

Dennis followed Loren through the kitchen door, looking confused. A few minutes later, we saw him stomp out, and I thought I would have to start looking for another cook. Then, Linda came to the rescue. She was good friends with June and was able to meet with them both and calm the situation. They stayed for the rest of the season.

Dennis served better eggs in time, but he was always a better artist than a cook. Linda and I talked him into painting a gold pan with a log cabin scene and creek. We paid him $150 for it and proudly display it in our home office to this day.

2000 and 2001 were good seasons for us. We were still mining good pay dirt and doing well. The relational problems at camp with Deed stayed the same, but we carried on like the stubborn Scandinavians we were. As far as Loren and I were concerned, we planned to continue mining, come hell or high water, and we weren't going to let a little squabbling sink a good operation! However, the price of gold was another matter.

*****

In 2002, the price of gold went down significantly, and Loren and I decided to let the equipment sit for the summer and find another source of income. Loren had recently built a house in Oshkosh and found a job working at Mercury, a watercraft engine builder and supplier. I accepted a position with an engineering company in North Bend, Washington, doing something completely different.

I was hired as a contractor to perform ground vibration monitoring at rock quarries and construction projects. I used portable seismographs to measure the vibrations and provide data of blasts in case anyone accused the company of causing damage to nearby structures, basement foundations, or environmental features because of the construction. Every other Friday, I would spend the morning in the field, setting up for the blast. I would videotape it and then spend the afternoon reporting on the seismographic activity.

One time, we worked in "Seattle Underground," a network of passages underneath Pioneer Square. There I saw remnants and artifacts of the bygone gold rush era up close. Another time in Olympia, we were blasting for a sewer project when they hit an area affected by a gas leak from years past. The charge lit up the leak with a remarkable spray of blue flame, streaming through the opening of the blast site. It was a total surprise, and we were lucky nobody got hurt. We also worked on a drilling project with Weyerhauser, in search of marketable gravel. That was a five-day job of collecting samples and preparing them for evaluation.

I enjoyed the blasting and even the work on site. The problem was the other days of the week. The boredom was torturous. They didn't have work for me, and I was basically required to report to the office and work as a "go-for" with pointless tasks and unnecessary requests. Otherwise, I spent my days looking at a bare desk. The whole situation felt wasteful. I didn't belong at a desk; I belonged on equipment. With nothing to do, I spent a lot of time daydreaming about returning to the Yukon and continuing work on the claims.

Eighteen months, I told myself. *I just have to stick it out for eighteen months.*

* * * * *

When 2003 rolled around, Loren told me he would stay in Wisconsin. I was disappointed but not surprised. He was still happy at Mercury then, and I know Deed wanted him home for the summer. When I told him I had all intention of going up alone, I could feel the hard feelings growing between us. We were partners, so we had to hash out an agreement about my activity at the mine, the use of equipment, yield, etc., knowing he would not be there. We were able to come to terms, and I reminded Loren that my presence at camp protected our investment. It wasn't safe to leave the equipment unmaintained and unattended for too long.

I returned to camp alone and worked for two weeks, preparing the equipment, and stripping the cut for the new year. As if my thought of vandalism had manifested itself, when I checked the engine oil in the 988, it was filled high above the full mark. I crawled under the machine with two five-gallon pails and drained nine gallons of water out of the crankcase before starting the engine. Had I started the machine up without checking, I could have seriously damaged it. The amount of water I drained was unprecedented. The only explanation I could think of was that someone had poured water into the engine to sabotage it. The D9H also had water in the transmission, but this didn't surprise me since the D9H was prone to problems taking on water.

I changed the oils in both machines and finished preparing the equipment for the season. I would never find out who may have tried to ruin my equipment, but I definitely had my suspicions. We were friends with our neighbors, but one of them was not to be trusted.

I had arranged for two men to help me since Loren was unavailable: Colin Greenough, who had previously worked with us, and Ted Tullis, who had mined locally but had shut down his operation a couple years prior. Ted was an excellent operator with great mechanical skills. They were not yet at camp when I arrived, so I had time to myself to strip the cut at the confluence of Discovery and Nansen Creeks. I worked long hours alone.

One night, it was about eight o'clock when I called it a day and began heading back to camp on my ATV. I rounded a corner, and about a hundred feet straight ahead in my road was a blond grizzly. The wind was in my face, so I had surprised him; he wasn't warned by my smell. Bears aren't known for their hearing, so he probably hadn't heard the ATV either. I slammed on the brake immediately, my heart pounding.

The old bear started dancing on all four legs, which meant he was irritated. I froze in fear, realizing I was in a perilous position. I was trapped on a strip of road too narrow to do a quick about-face. I was on high ground. On one side was a small, narrow creek and a steep ditch on the other. The ditch was the lesser of the two evils, but it would take some driving finesse and time to pull out quickly. I could put the bear at an advantage if he walked over. Even if I did manage to turn around and tear out of there, grizzlies are the fastest bears and can run up to thirty-five miles per hour if they wanted. My ATV only went forty-five. I would need a great head start to outrun him. Without a gun, my only option was to wait and see what the bear wanted.

But he kept dancing, keeping his eye on me. Sometimes he turned away, but not long enough for me to make a break for it. After what seemed like hours, he dropped his formidable paws to the ground, lifted his nose in the air, and lumbered off in a completely different direction. I saw this as my chance. As quickly as I could, I backed into the ditch and pulled the ATV out as quickly as I could. I'm sure he heard my engine rev and peel out as I floored the accelerator and fled.

When I felt far enough away and my heart began to slow just a bit, I stopped and looked over my shoulder. The bear was not in pursuit but standing on his hind legs again and watching my exit. He wasn't in the mood to chase me. What a lucky break.

When I was further up the road, I returned to the machine I had been operating and spent another hour working until I was sure the danger was past. This was my most dangerous encounter with a grizzly, and I'm grateful I'm alive to tell about it. An unpredictable grizzly is a miner's biggest fear when working in the bush. Being alone made it even more dangerous.

The following year, Loren had a similar encounter with a grizzly. He was also on his ATV driving back toward camp when he spotted a mama grizzly with her cub—one of the most dangerous bear encounters to have. He was on a hill and a narrow road, and, like me, he managed to stay still and calm, to pose no threat to the pair. Mama and baby kept up their foraging, then walked away, uninterested in Loren.

The next year, we were determined to have guns at camp. Canada allowed them, but expected you to register them every sixty days, which would have involved several expensive, time-consuming trips into Skagway. We managed to get two twelve-gauge shotguns to camp and kept them strapped to the side of our ATV. Once we had protection, we never encountered a bear again!

*****

In line with my ongoing bad history with cooks, the first cook I hired in 2003 disappointed us. His name was Darryl, and he was a young native out of cooking school in Whitehorse and seemed like a winner. He cooked for us very well for one week, then didn't show up again until Tuesday. We had lost a lot of time cooking for ourselves on Monday, and I was peeved. He thought I was taking his absence all too seriously and laughed off his long weekend. I fired him on the spot for his attitude and replaced him with Earl, an older gentleman, who stayed with us the whole summer.

My home for 2003 was the old Coachman fifth wheel trailer that Linda and I had shared back in 1995. It was plenty big enough for me. Work and motherhood would keep Linda at home that summer, although she insisted that I call her every night using the satellite phone. I had told her about the bear, and she wanted to know I was safe. That summer, we racked up a thousand-dollar phone bill every month.

Our old friend Bruce Wheeler was now the watchman and manager of the closed BYG hard rock mine. Bruce lived in the main administration building, which had also been the kitchen for the crews when the mine was in operation. With full access to the kitchen and dining room, Bruce's wife, Grace, Bruce's sister-in-law, Twyla, and Bruce's sister, Marcy, treated the community to a "salmon bake." They invited twenty or so miners from the area. They served salmon several different ways: baked, grilled, and smoked, with several varieties of each, all trimmed with several types of potatoes and vegetables. Everything was memorably delicious, and those recipes and cooking methods have undoubtedly been passed down through the family since that first salmon bake. We were so grateful for the Wheeler family's generosity and the opportunity to socialize with different miners in the area and exchange ideas and stories.

Loren and I had an alarming conversation one evening at a Salmon Bake with a medical doctor from Whitehorse. The doctor told us it was critical not to get hurt at camp because if we needed medical attention, he was not allowed to treat us because we were Americans. It was sobering news to hear because injury is always possible in our business. We were very cautious and, fortunately, no one at camp ever required medical attention.

*****

In 2004, the price of gold rose again. Loren was dissatisfied with his work in Oshkosh, so he accompanied me to the Yukon. It was so good to have him back. We were always at our best when we were together, and this year it was just the two of us.

Linda would come and go that summer, depending on Kelsey's schedule. Being older now, Kelsey had little interest in coming to camp and being away from friends for the summer. When Linda was there, she would make tasty meals for us and freeze them for us to eat throughout the summer.

Deed took her time getting to camp that year. Linda had been there cooking, cleaning, and doing laundry for about five weeks before Deed flew in. The three of us drove to town to pick her up. On the way home, we stopped at a grocery store and bought a chicken dinner with all the trimmings. We stopped at the Fox Lake campground, a beautiful spot between Whitehorse and the mine, at the picnic area near the water's edge. It was a picture-perfect, clear summer day. We relaxed and chatted together, enjoying nature's bounty and appreciating the soaring mountains, crystalline lake, and fragrant pines. In that moment, I thought of how happy we were there, the four of us, together, getting along. And I wondered why it couldn't always be that way. I dared to hope that this might be the year things would be different.

Meanwhile, back at the mine, we stripped a new cut in an area where BYG built the first settling ponds on our lowest claim on Nansen Creek. We stripped on the left limit to the center of the valley. The strippings had to be hauled over a large tailings pile, which took extra time and fuel. We had years of tailing pond slime to move out of our way. It was a reasonably small cut compared to the last two years, but because we were limited in stripping space, we decided to divide it and mine half in 2004 and the other in 2005.

Loren and I pulled the wash plant down to the new cut and set it on top of the tailings from previous years. We used an existing settling pond for water discharge. The ground was good and had plenty of gold to give us a fairly good season.

*****

Our existing Land Use and Water Permit expired in July of 2005. Loren had volunteered to work on the permit application for us since I had been doing the bookkeeping. I was glad he took it on. Unfortunately, though, we didn't submit our application until mid-March of 2005, and it took several months to approve it. For most of the first half of the summer, we were not allowed to discharge any water from our mining operation. Loren and I spent several weeks working on our equipment and completed all the low-priority maintenance tasks that had been on the back burner for some time.

We also looked at future mining claims above Discovery Creek on Nansen. We brought the 235 to the area and started a prospect trench across the valley. The ground was permafrost, and Loren spent time every day for a month scratching the thawed material until we found the pay layer. It panned well, and we decided to mine the upper claims. We finished prospecting just in time to receive our new permit on July 15.

We immediately got to work sluicing. We had the rest of the season to work on the remaining claim under the old ponds. The pay was good, and we were very pleased with our production. This claim was one of the best in our claim group because the gold ran across the entire floor of the valley. The claim was just below the confluence and Nansen and Dolly Creek. The refiner told us the assay of our gold on our Nansen claim was higher, indicating the major portion of higher quality gold was coming from another source, Dolly.

There was a lot of work to do for the 2006 season. It's always difficult to open a new area and begin mining. We had finished prospecting and liked what we saw, but we had a lot of stripping and drainage work to do. There were many things to consider, including stripping space, covering future pay dirt, setting the plant, and other issues. Loren and I had a saying, "If it isn't in your HEAD, it's in your BACK." That means if you don't think things through, you'll eventually have more physical work to do. In other words, planning is critical to maximize productivity and minimize waste both in time and fuel.

In 2006, we arrived in the Yukon in mid-April, expecting a difficult time moving the organic, black, frozen muck, but we didn't expect so much glacier ice. Glacier ice was common on Nansen Creek, and the valley in this area had a large sheet of it in 2006. We ripped it, stacked it, and hauled it off the cut using the 988. The loader was slow and lumbered over the rough ground ominously. Fortunately, we finished stripping the cut before the muck softened and became impossible to remove. Then we pulled the wash plant a mile up to our new mining site. We used the D9H but saved wear and tear on the machine by pushing it with the mighty 988. The D9H stood on its heels under the pull. The cut gave us a tough time, but in the end, it paid well and opened up ground for future mining above Discovery Creek.

* * * * *

In 2007, Loren and I both purchased generators. I found an eighty-kilowatt, three-phase generator to power the wash plant, and Loren found a twenty-kilowatt generator to power the camp. The generator Loren found had survived a fire, but the damaged components had been repaired or replaced. The new generators replaced our older, smaller generators, which we could now keep as backups.

The eighty kilowatt one I found had a sturdy 3404 Cat engine with serious issues. I bought it from a farmer who got it from the phone company. It was a backup generator with only 450 hours. They told me they had operated it briefly on the farm. I hauled it to the Yukon, assuming we could make minor repairs to get it running. Loren and I worked for a few days and discovered the fuel system had been contaminated with water for an extended period. The seller had lied to me; he had not operated the generator for years.

We weren't about to give up. We took it to Finning Cat in Whitehorse to get it running, then to a place called Independent Electric because it was only putting out three volts instead of the 440 volts necessary to power our wash plant. We spent a bit of time and money on that generator, but it worked well once restored.

During the winter of 2007, I traveled to Carson City to visit the builder and designer of the IRD jig we had been using to clean our gold for many years. They had developed a new stainless-steel screen to allow more coarse gold to pass through during the jigging process, and Loren and I wanted to try it.

One day, I was on the Cat bulldozer stripping while Loren changed the screen. He had the harder job since the jig hadn't been taken apart for years. He had to wrestle loose parts that were pieces cemented together by dried liquid concentrates. It was time-consuming work. Suddenly, I saw Loren trying to get my attention. I was more than ready for a break, so I powered down the Cat and walked over to him.

"I've got something to show you," he said, motioning me to follow him.

He led me into the shipping container where we had set up the jig to clean gold away from the weather. The original screen deck was off.

"Look inside," he said.

I peered inside, and even in the dim light, I could see the twinkle of gold flashing off the sides of the metal machine. Over the years, the concentrates had attached to the inside walls of the jig hutch, and then attracted more bits of concentrate. We could see that the total accumulation inside the jig and the wealth of gold therein was considerable. In fact, the depth of the amassed concentrate was nearly an inch thick. We had never thought to clean the inside, especially because the concentrate was supposed to pass through the screen, then easily slide through the chamber and discharge into our waiting container. Still, we were all smiles and couldn't believe our good fortune! When we finished cleaning the gold from the concentrate, we had uncovered thirty-two troy ounces! This discovery was exciting and impeccably timed. We greatly needed startup funds for the new cut.

*****

From 2008 to 2012, Loren and I typically worked alone. It was a period of equipment upgrades, beginning with our 2008 adventure trying to buy an excavator.

Upon surveying what we had left to mine, we decided we could be more efficient with larger equipment. We purchased a Cat 245 excavator from a dealer in Fairbanks. The machine was in Chico, California, so we had it trucked to Seattle and left at the dock of Alaska Marine Lines, where it was eventually loaded onto a barge and hauled to Skagway. It was hard to find a trucking company with a heavy enough trailer to haul it to the mine. We had found the right trucker, but when he got to Skagway, he found that the excavator's undercarriage was in its extended position, making the machine too wide for him to load and haul safely. He called and asked to have the track frames retracted to narrow the carbody. Loren and I collected our tools, loaded them into our truck, and prepared for the six-hour drive to Skagway to modify the excavator.

Skagway is a small town of about one thousand people with a busy Alaska port that serves all of the Yukon Territory through Seattle and Vancouver. Everything arrives through Skagway, including our excavator. We checked into the hotel, had dinner, and then got a good night's sleep. We expected a problematic next day because we didn't have our one-inch air impact wrench or a good portable air compressor to power it. We knew we were looking at loosening sixty-four large, one-inch bolts before adjusting the track frames on the excavator. We had our breaker bars and sockets and hoped they would be enough to do the job.

When we arrived at the dock the following day, Alaska Marine Lines offered us the use of a 966 Cat loader to push the track frames after we removed the bolts. I don't know what we would have done without that machine! We removed the bolts, slid the track frames in, then re-bolted and secured the track frames in one ten-hour day. We called the driver back so he could start his trek to the mine with the excavator. There were two trucks to haul the 245—the main frame on one load and the counterweight, boom, stick, and bucket on the second load. The next morning, we helped load and chain the machine to the trailer, then left for the mine via Whitehorse.

It took a few days to set up the 245. The dealer sent us a narrow trenching bucket because we didn't specify we wanted a general-purpose bucket. They took full advantage of our error to send the more inefficient bucket. We planned on using the 245 for mass excavating and baling pay dirt, so we had to order a new, reasonably priced, sixty-inch, general purpose bucket from Grand Prairie, Alberta. We were able to ship it to Whitehorse and bring it out to the creek. Then, we machined five-inch pins and spacers to fit into the 245. The extra steel and machine work added up, but the bucket was new, and we were confident in the machine's value.

However, after 225 hours of work with the 245, we already saw excessive wear on the bucket. At 250 hours, Loren was digging in some hard ground when the cutting edge peeled right off the bucket ending its ability to dig! We jumped off our machines and inspected the crumpled metal laying in the dirt. The bucket had been poorly constructed in China. We snapped a few pictures and sent them to the dealer. They offered to send us a good used general-purpose bucket if we paid the freight from Grand Prairie. We agreed and soon we were back in business.

With the machine's help, we had a productive year.

*****

In 2010, we hired a company that was using geophysical surveys to determine the bedrock depth on our creeks. For twenty years, we had been told by geologists who had studied the earth in the area that the richest deposits were in the true bedrock, and we had been mining a false bedrock (boulder clay). We also knew the land had been glaciated twice. We wanted to know how deep we needed to dig to hit bedrock.

The survey company determined the approximate depth to bedrock through electromagnetic induction. They ran two lines of electrical sensors across the width of our claims: one on the lower and upper claims. The sensors detected changes in electrical conductivity that would occur at the interface between soil and bedrock to determine the depth. The line on the lower claims revealed the true bedrock was about ninety feet from the surface. The line on the upper claim revealed bedrock at fifty feet. We were optimistic we could strip the upper claim and finally know the pay value of the true bedrock. The information could help us sell the claim with the reserves.

Loren and I decided exploring the deeper ground was in our best interest. We opened a small cut 100 by 200 feet and started to dig. Then we hit glacier till, the fine, silty sediment left behind by glaciers that never contains gold. After so much work, we were very disappointed. I ripped the till and pushed it to Loren to dig out of the hole, then used the front-end loader to haul it away. By the time we began hauling the till with the loaders, it had turned into a nearly impossible sloppy slurry, and we struggled to get rid of it. We had set a six-inch pump in the hole to dewater the cut, which we kept running twenty-four hours a day. We used the construction truck with the telescoping boom to move the pump as needed on our way down.

We managed to get forty-five feet deep where we should have been getting near the pay layer. All we could find was more till. We ripped and dug a test hole to see if we were anywhere near the pay zone. Ten feet down, we only found more till. Discouraged and defeated after spending two weeks and $50,000 in our efforts to find gold, we shut down the exploration project. We moved to shallower ground to recover our losses.

We decided to drill to determine if we had any pay on the left limit (east side) of Nansen Creek on our lower claims. We hired a driller from Whitehorse when he was in the area to see if we could find true bedrock above Discovery Creek near our deep excavation project. The driller made a hole eighty-five feet deep where we were told the bedrock was fifty feet deep. All we found was more glacial till. We were very thankful we had terminated our deep excavation when we did.

2010 was also the year we could see the undercarriage was about finished on our trusty Cat DH9. The old girl was getting tired. We needed to invest in a new undercarriage or buy another bulldozer. Loren and I discussed it and decided to look for a machine that could dependably finish the work we had ahead of us.

We worked with the salesman at Finning Cat to find us a machine in the affordable range, ready to work. He suggested a D9N tractor from Smithers, British Columbia. I flew up to Smithers to look the Cat over as best I could because it was in pieces, about to be reassembled. It seemed in good condition, and we trusted the seller that the machine would work well for us. We asked him for a few modifications, which he agreed to do, and we purchased the machine and paid to have it trucked to Whitehorse.

*****

It was late February in 2011 and well below zero when the machine arrived in Whitehorse. The fuel had gelled in transit. The D9N wouldn't start, so it could not be unloaded from the truck. They parked the heavy haul truck inside a bay to let it warm up before continuing to the dealer.

Loren and I arranged to have the tractor delivered in the spring of 2011 before the road restrictions were in effect. When the mechanics went to start the D9N, they discovered the coolant had dropped into the engine crankcase. They figured the heat exchanger had failed and changed it, confident they had repaired the problem. However, when the D9N arrived on the creek, we went up to start the machine and pulled the engine oil dipstick. Again, we had coolant in the engine crankcase.

Wearily, we changed the oil and started the Cat, hoping the warmer weather would help the machine run long enough for us to decide what repairs were needed. We opened the battery box, ready to reconnect the battery. The trucker had disconnected it after transit to avoid any voltage leaks. Now, the batteries were gone and obviously stolen!

Unfortunately, we suspected the thief was one of our neighbors. We confirmed it when we visited his machine and noticed two batteries that fit our equipment in his Cat excavator. At first, we weren't too upset because we figured the batteries in the used piece of equipment were probably older anyway. When Finning told us they had installed new batteries at $400 each, we weren't happy at all. However, we felt it best not to confront our neighbor. He was a friend, and it would have been his word against ours. Again, our goal in the Yukon was peace at any price.

Finally, the machine seemed ready to go with new oil and batteries, a good blade, a ripper, and all her jewelry. We started it up, and noticed oil pouring out of one of the main lift cylinders as we lifted the ripper. We had no choice but to shut it down, remove the lift cylinder, and have it rebuilt in Whitehorse. We couldn't believe it. Another disappointment that should have been declared by the seller! The cylinder was probably leaking when the machine left Smithers.

It cost $5,000 to repair the cylinder. Once installed on the tractor again, we thought we could finally start work. Then, as we began rolling it toward the creek and the cut, we heard a horrible, buzzing sound. We just couldn't catch a break. The transmission/power train warning was flashing, and the warning buzzer was buzzing. We stopped work, replaced the filters, and started up again. A few hours later, the warning system informed us of a problem with the powertrain.

Our hearts sank. Taking the machine apart on the creek to repair the powertrain was impossible. We needed to be enclosed in a shop to keep sand and dirt out of the components. We called Finning, removed the blade and ripper, and trucked the Cat to Whitehorse for work.

By now, it was June. Finning completely dissembled the D9 and found that the failure was caused by the previous owner's final drive failure. The previous owner had pulled the failed final drive out and installed a new one without cleaning the transmission housing. They then put a coat of paint on the machine and listed it for sale. Missing this major step set us up for a major component failure. All the steel from the final failure had circulated through the power train, taking out the transmission pump, torque converter, transmission bearings, and all related interior drive train components. We had trusted the seller and equipment salesman. If they had taken the time to clean the contaminants after the final drive failure, we would have saved so much expense and downtime.

Making matters worse, Finning now had a delay in ordering the parts they needed for our repair because of a recent changeover in their computer system. Instead of a three-week job, the tractor lay in pieces in their shop until December, when they could get the parts and finish the repair. We said goodbye to the D9N for the season.

* * * * *

In 2011, Deed arrived at the camp a week before Linda. On arrival, Deed's mission was to paint the cabin she and Loren shared. Deed sent me into town with a four-page grocery list. At the hotel, Linda and I were adding things that we liked to the list when I posted on Facebook how happy I was to have Linda coming out to camp and how I appreciated her cooking. Loren and I had been foraging for ourselves except for a pulled pork meal Deed had prepared for us shortly after she arrived. We had been eating the pulled pork for three days until Loren put what was left in the freezer; we couldn't eat it any longer. I'm not quite sure how my words were taken out of context, but when Linda and I returned to camp, it was obvious Deed had seen the post and interpreted it as complaining about the cooking in camp.

Everything "hit the fan." Deed had been looking for conflict, and now she had it. She was angry, so Loren became angry at me as well. Deed drove to Whitehorse the next day and mysteriously spent $1,000 on household items. Two days later, she left camp with the household items and returned to Wisconsin. Apparently, she had been shopping for a house in Texas and went down to buy it while Loren was on the creek with us. That was the end of Deed's days at camp. I felt terrible for Loren, but relieved that Deed's negative presence at camp was gone. I didn't realize I would not see or speak to her for another five years.

* * * * *

On a cold day in January 2012, I received the call that our tractor had been completely rebuilt and was ready to go. Finning would store the tractor in their yard until we could move it back up to Nansen Creek in March before the road weight restrictions went into effect.

Unfortunately, when we finally had the tractor working for the season, we realized the heat exchanger did not fix problems we were still seeing. We concluded that coolant was migrating past the liners under the heads. The engine needed a major overhaul. We had

Finning mechanics come to the mine and pull the engine out. We loaded it onto our truck and hauled it into Whitehorse to their shop to rebuild.

A few weeks later, two mechanics came back to install the engine into the tractor onsite. We thought it might be a two-day job, but the crackerjacks had it running at 1:30 in the morning. I know this because I was awakened by the sound of a revving engine. They went to bed and finished putting the tractor together in the morning. Finally, it was ready to go to work after rebuilding it from radiator to ripper. We didn't expect to invest so much in it, but we had a fine tractor to finish our mining plan.

With the 245 and the D9N, Loren and I could handle more dirt between us. Sometimes we were both on the bulldozers, and other times, on the excavators. We had enough equipment and backups if any machine needed repair. We finished 2012 well and quickly, thanks to our new equipment.

*****

After 2012, it was clear my mining career with Loren was winding down. I was still engaged, but Loren's lack of interest was growing. I was eager to leave for the mine in the spring and get started, but Loren was much less enthused. I know he was caught in a tug-of-war between Deed and me every summer. Soon, I found myself going up at the regular dates in the spring and for two years, I went up alone and hired help to get the year underway. I don't think I understood how much pressure he was under at the time. Deed wanted him to stop, and he wanted to keep working with me. Neither Deed nor I could entertain a compromise solution.

Loren was also beginning to struggle physically with the work. He would avoid the more strenuous tasks, like feeding the plant, which often required dislodging rocks stuck between the grizzly bars. Sometimes they had to be broken, which meant getting on top of the feeder with a twenty-pound sledgehammer and breaking them into small pieces.

Loren also realized the danger in our work and could see how we were playing a young man's game. We reduced our daily working hours and left earlier in the fall.

Looking back, I regret not realizing Loren's dilemma and what the stress was doing to him. One night, when we were relaxing after work, he turned to me with serious eyes.

"You know I'm 61, the same age dad was when he died," he began.

I nodded slowly, reading his mind.

"I want to have time to enjoy my retirement before I leave this life," he finished.

I understood what he was saying and what it meant for me. My days mining with Loren were numbered. But what that number was had yet to be determined.

CHAPTER 11

HEART'S PARTINGS

Few people have ever had the privilege of holding a gold bar in their hands. Even fewer have ever had the privilege of creating a gold bar.

We began melting our gold and pouring it into bars out of necessity around 2011. For years, we had been giving our gold dust in plastic bottles to the representative in Whitehorse to forward to Technic Canada, our refiner. Given the submission process, we knew we probably had a net loss of three percent. Melting our own gold gave us a baseline for consistency between the refiner and us.

It would take three to four hours to heat the furnace to twenty-one hundred degrees to get a good melt. Then, we placed the gold dust into the crucible with the flux, which is the substance you add to the melt that helps float the impurities out of the placer gold. Many different things can be used for flux, but we used soda ash. It would take about thirty minutes for our gold to liquify. The melt color was a bright yellow since our gold contained fifteen to sixteen percent silver. It was a beautiful sight! Then we would carefully pour it into the bar mold where it would quickly begin to solidify.

After a surprisingly short time, we could pop it out of the mold and into cold water until it was cool to the touch. The molded bars were covered with slag, the impurities that surfaced during the melt. The slag was like a hard, brittle cap on the poured bar which we would chip away with a light hammer, then use a wire brush to polish and reveal the bright yellow gold beneath.

Holding a gold bar is an incredible feeling, and it was a surreal paycheck for all our hard work. We drilled a hole in every bar before turning it into the refiner. This enabled us to keep an assay record of the gold by saving the small, drilled sample. It was a happy day when our gold bars went off to the refiner because we knew we were earning as much as possible for all our hard work.

We showed Mom photos of our beautiful gold bars, but it's a shame she never got to hold one in her hands after all those years of cleaning gold. She was in her twilight years and living in an assisted living facility near my sister Karen in Raleigh, North Carolina.

Linda and I had found a lovely place to live in Sparks, Nevada. In the off-season, we alternated between that home and a condominium in Puerto Vallarta we had purchased in 2004. Linda had an uncle in the area, and we fell in love with PV on our first visit there. We loved both our homes, but as far as I was concerned, the mining camp was just as dear to me.

*****

In a placer mining operation, the sluice box is considered sacred. There is an unwritten law that miners must respect the equipment of each other's operations. We had private access to our mining claims, wash plant, and sluice box for years. Then in 2014, we had a new neighbor next to our claim. His name was Karl Chassian, and he was a tough Russian and a world-class cusser. His wife was Mennonite, and we often saw her in her bonnet and long dress. They owned five claims below us, and we were friendly and helpful to him through the years.

To get to our plant, one had to drive right through our camp. Therefore, our sluice box was secure. However, one evening, around eleven o'clock, I heard a four-wheeler pass my trailer while lying in bed. I registered it as unusual in my sleepy state but nothing to wake over. Karl had noticed it, too, when it got closer to his camp. He also saw that the driver did not have his lights on as the ATV headed up the road toward the BVG hard rock mine. Karl grew suspicious. Karl's sluice box was more accessible than ours because the road system triangulated, so someone could stealthily gain access, especially in the middle of the night!

Karl immediately jumped into his car and took the shortcut to his sluice box. Then he shut the car off and waited to see if the phantom ATV rider would be paying a visit. Karl heard the ATV coming towards him, slowing down as it drew closer to the sluice box. Karl steeled himself for battle, but then his foot slipped, and he accidentally touched the brakes. The brake lights streamed through the dark night. The ATV turned and accelerated, tearing back up to the Dolly Creek cabin he came from, which Karl knew was part of a Chinese operation in the area. The driver's very suspicious behavior left no doubt that he intended to raid the sluice box. Karl followed the ATV back to the Dolly Creek cabin and went to the door.

He knocked on it with a gun in hand and told the intruder, "If I catch you down near my sluice box again, this is the gun I'm going to shoot you with."

The next day, the intruder drove into Carmacks and filed a complaint against Karl with the Royal Canadian Mounted Police. They came out with a SWAT Team and held Karl and his family at gunpoint, removing the five weapons that Karl had in camp. A court date was set for Karl to appear and plead his case before a judge. This is just one example of the ways the Canadian government tried to police the "wild west" attitude among the miners, but it wasn't easy. Miners put their heart and soul into their operations and used their gut instincts and constant vigilance to protect their resources.

For example, we had to replace the belt on our belt feeder many times throughout our mining years. We always saved our "takeoff" belting in the "boneyard," where we kept all our used parts. The used belting would often come in handy for different projects. We often had trouble replacing our worn belting because it was hard to find quality, reliable belting in Whitehorse. We ultimately found the toughest we could in Superior, Wisconsin, through our friend Herbert James, who supervised a taconite loading facility. He offered us used belting for free, which Loren would cut to width and length and prepare the belt for installation before shipping it the three thousand miles from Wisconsin to Whitehorse. We stored our roll of used belting in the boneyard with other spare parts until we needed it.

Karl came to us one day and asked if he could have a piece of old belting to replace his damaged one until he could get to

Whitehorse to buy a replacement. In the placer miner spirit, I told Karl he was welcome to one of the used belts in the boneyard, and we went about our work. After a few minutes, a strange, uneasy feeling came over me. I asked Loren to come with me to see how Karl was doing. When we arrived, we saw Karl had already unrolled our unused belt from Wisconsin and was about to start cutting it to size to fit his smaller belt feeder. Had we been five minutes late, our spare belt, which we had been so painstakingly prepared and shipped for our use, would have been cut and made completely useless.

Another time, on upper Nansen and Summit Creek, the new Chinese mine owners were considering expanding access to their mine. All they had was a long, time-consuming, rough road over a mountain ridge. We had mined our claims on Nansen and had built a very good road to the top of our claims adjacent to his lowest claim. Our wash plant screened the tailings which gave us nice gravel to cap our roads.

One day, the mine owner, David, visited us. He asked to build a road to our claims from his lower claim and use our road for better access for his operation. We sympathized with his situation and intention but had to decline his request. If we allowed access through our claims to his, we would lose all control of outsider access to our sluice box. A few days later, we noticed an excavator working on our top claim. Loren and I didn't waste any time in taking our ATVs up to talk with the excavator operator. He told us David had sent him to build the road onto our claims. We told him to cease work; the road wasn't going to happen. Luckily, David respected our words, and we never saw their excavator on our claim again.

When we finished mining the upper claims, we went into high gear with our reclamation responsibilities. The upper claims were mined under our more recent permit, which required covering the excavated area with black topsoil. We recreated a gradual rock and gravel meandering stream bed and graded the topsoil to allow natural plants to revegetate the mined area.

We moved our wash plant downstream and started stripping and sluicing some side pay on the east side of the valley. We had stripped as much material as possible on the east side slope, and surprisingly, it had helped thaw the permafrost under the strippings. Stripping was easier because we could push the material downhill, saving us time and fuel. We stripped a reasonably deep bench thirty to fifty feet deep, but the pay could have been better. Fortunately for us, the price of gold had increased, and with our low overhead (just the two of us working), we still yielded a profit. We also had several good settling ponds from previous work in the area and were able to rejuvenate them to accept effluent discharge from our sluicing process.

We set up the wash plant in the center of a two-thousand-foot stretch of the bench intending to mine the entire section of bench pay. Half of the pay was below the plant, while the other half was upstream of the wash plant. Our Cat 988 loader could haul the pay one thousand feet and keep up with the one hundred yards per hour pace we needed to feed our plant.

Loren and I spent our last four years working the marginal ground. We made a solid living, but we took a lot of risk for the small amount of gold we recovered. Maybe we both knew it was the best we would do at that stage of our mining careers or perhaps we were more comfortable with life and didn't feel the need to push as hard as we once did. Either way, we were satisfied with our mining efforts and pressed on.

*****

The second of the original miners in the Johnson Mining Company left this earth on May 5, 2016. Loren and I were home when we got word from my sister, Karen, who lived near Mom's nursing facility, that Mom had passed. The family considerately arranged for a memorial in September, at the end of our mining season.

Townspeople gathered from near and far to say goodbye to Phyllis Johnson. We held the memorial at our home church, Mission Covenant, in Poplar. As a tribute to Mom, Karen and Brenda baked three hundred of Mom's signature cinnamon rolls for those who attended the service.

I had seen been with Loren for the last five summers mining, but the memorial service was the first time I had seen Deed in five years. We didn't talk at all, and I was disappointed when neither she nor Loren accompanied the family to the graveside service where we said our final goodbyes to Mom. This end of an era for the Johnson family sadly correlated with the closing of our mine. The funeral was like a tolling bell, signaling the end of our enterprise.

Loren had told me at the beginning of the summer that 2016 would be his last season, and I accepted his resignation. I understood the pressure he was under from Deed. Linda had been patient and understanding for a long time, but she, too, was then pressuring me to retire and spend more time at home.

Our final mining season was fraught with unpleasant events. Our torque converter on the 988B started to give out as we hurried to get our pay to the wash plant. We found an option to rent a Cat rock truck from a neighbor miner near us on Back Creek and hired our friend Ed Wheeler to help us operate it. We also met the limit on the tracks of the Cat D9N, and I parked it with the tracks so worn it would push no more until the rails were replaced. Loren was so disgruntled he refused to spend a dime repairing the Cat undercarriage or the 988. We parked them both and finished the season with the smaller loaders and the old tired D9H.

On the very last day of the season, I was running the D9H to finish some reclamation work. I put the bulldozer in reverse to park it for the winter and felt something unusual. I looked at my left track and saw it had split, and I was walking out of it. The timing was unbelievable, and my frustration level couldn't have been higher. In a few hours, we had the track repaired, and the machine was ready to go again. We parked it and winterized it for next season. At least we had some working equipment to throw into the bargain when we sold the mine.

We also knew if we were selling our mine claims, we needed to locate our claim posts on Discovery Creek, where we had prospected but never mined. Loren and I spent an afternoon on our ATVs and on foot, traveling up Discovery Creek to locate the posts on our nine claims. The tundra was hard to navigate in many areas, and we were both exhausted by the end of the day.

Finally, we were down to searching for the last claim post. I trekked near the creek while Loren went to search the upper area near our ATVs. I found the claim stake near the creek and marked it with surveyor's tape. Then, as I made my way back to Loren, I suddenly saw a dark figure on the ground up ahead. It was Loren.

I ran to him and found him conscious but feeling very sick. I asked him what was wrong, but he didn't have a good answer.

"Go ahead back to camp," he said. "I'll be along later."

"I'm not leaving you here alone," I replied, thinking about our previous encounters with grizzly bears. A weakened human makes an easy meal, and we were two miles from camp. "I'll stay with you until you feel better," I added.

I still don't know what debilitated Loren that day, but he clearly had some health issues he didn't care to share with me. So instead, we spent the time talking about work. Our investigation into the claim posts showed that the miner owning the claims above us had been prospecting on our claims and had even moved the claim posts!

After a short time, Loren felt better, and we returned to camp. We wasted no time calling the mining inspector to enter the claims and locate the legal posts and claim borders. Our inspector, Matt, spent the day with an assistant from his office and located and marked the legal and original claim stakes. We were relieved to know the size of our claims and their value to the mine.

In preparation for closing our operation, we also did our final gold cleanup. For the past fifteen years, Loren and I had saved black sands with gold dust as fine as flour that could not be recovered in our regular jigging process. Now, with our reclamation finished and our mining duties concluded, we had the time to try different ways to separate the gold. We had purchased a magnetic separator in Oregon, and now we modified the jig to use it. We processed about four cubic yards of black sand concentrates through the jig and managed to recover ninety percent of the bulk out of the black sands in a couple of days. To catch the last ten percent, we had more cleanup methods, including a vibrating table designed to separate very fine gold dust from the remaining black sand. The table cleaning process was speedy and efficient and resulted in relatively clean concentrate.

We recovered any remaining gold using the gold wheel. Our time and effort cleaning the black sand rewarded us with only twelve troy ounces of clean gold. This made us realize how efficiently the IRD jig operated throughout the many years we had used it.

Loren had published an ad for the sale of the mine on an online site. There was nothing I could do to stop him, and I knew it was the nail in the coffin of our mine operation. Then, as we were doing our final gold cleanup, two interested buyers stopped to see us from Alberta. We spent the afternoon with them, and Loren gave them a tour. They expressed sincere interest and returned a few days later just to talk and look again at our operation. The pair were serious and financially capable of the purchase. David, who was better known as "Rabbit," his CB handle, was in the trucking business and a successful oil field service contractor. Torr was an equipment heavy hauler, also from the oil patch. Torr had an unusually deep voice which seemed fitting for his name. Linda coined him, "Torr of the North." They left in high spirits and told us they would be in touch.

With the gold cleaned and ready for market, the claim status legally established and staked, and even some potential buyers in contact with us, it was time to close the camp for good. We worked stoically, realizing our actions meant the end of our thirty-five years as partners, working and living together towards a singular goal. We also knew we would return to the creek only to tie up loose ends and move on. I knew I would have to accept a life without mining, or at least a life without mining with Loren.

When it was time to pull out for the last time, we said unceremonious goodbyes and went our separate ways—Loren to Texas and I to Nevada. My heart was heavy. I was confident we would find buyers, but the thought was a meager substitute for no longer working together.

*****

During the winter months of 2017, Loren and I engaged in ongoing negotiations with the pair of Alberta oil tycoons. We supplied as much information as possible to help them decide, and their interest was unwavering. The price of oil had dropped considerably, and they were eager to try something new. By now, gold mining had entered the popular consciousness, thanks to cable television shows like *Gold Rush, Prospectors,* and *Yukon Gold.* I thought these "reality" shows showed anything but the reality of gold mining and concentrated on trumped-up drama and unrealistic outcomes. They failed to show the hard work, sacrifice, and knowledge base it took to make a mining operation profitable. However, Torr watched them religiously and thought gold mining would be as easy as they made it look on television.

Simultaneously, a couple from Carmacks with a group of Chinese buyers contacted me with an interest in the buying the mine. Many Chinese groups were buying existing mines in the Mount Nansen drainage area, so their interest was sincere and needed to be taken seriously. While I was working with the Chinese group, Loren continued negotiations with the Alberta buyers. However, I soon saw Loren's desperation to close the deal and be done with the whole thing. I informed my Chinese group that we had made the sale. We hired an attorney and hammered out the details, which included a special clause. Rabbit and Torr asked Loren and I to commit to three weeks in the spring of 2017 to help them transition as new mine operators. Loren and I discussed it, and because we sincerely wanted them to be successful, we agreed to do so. After all, they were new to mining and had a lot to learn.

After the second week, Rabbit made me an offer that was impossible to refuse. He asked if I would be willing to stay on for the rest of the summer and continue guiding them through the steep learning curve. I talked it over with Linda, and she agreed to give it one more summer. Linda was not happy when she was appointed by Rabbit to be the camp cook, and I was so grateful to have her patience and support in this crazy life I loved, right to the bittersweet end. I realized I could have bought Loren out, but truthfully, I never considered it for a moment. I simply wasn't interested in running the mine without Loren. I couldn't even imagine it.

The next week, Loren's three-week commitment was finished. The day before Loren left for Whitehorse to meet Deed for the drive back, he and I were invited to the annual barbeque at Finning Caterpillar. We were among friends we had worked with for years and people who had been so integral to our success: mechanics, salespeople, office personnel, and, of course, the branch manager. However, there was a strange distance between Loren and me. We hardly made eye contact or exchanged words the entire time we were at the event. It was just a very uncomfortable time for both of us after working together for all those years. We were both facing our individual unknowns.

The next day, Loren, Linda, and I left for Whitehorse to tie up some last-minute business. Deed was flying into Whitehorse late that evening to accompany Loren home to Texas. We left Nansen Creek at different times, as we had our own trucks. When we arrived, Linda and I went to the hotel room and talked about the upcoming big life change and what was in store for me and Loren. It was hard to find words to describe the day, but sadness was an overriding emotion for me. It was getting close to dinnertime when Linda had a great idea. Deed hadn't arrived yet and Loren was alone.

"Why don't we invite Loren to dinner with us?" she suggested. I agreed, and we invited Loren to meet us at our favorite restaurant, Klondike Rib and Salmon. Our dinner conversation was very comfortable, but at the same time, we were all saddened to know this was the end of our many years working shoulder to shoulder. I think Loren was very happy we had this time together; Linda and I certainly were. The hardest part was saying goodbye as we looked into each other's mutually sad eyes. After our lifetime of work and adventure, working as closely as two people can, Loren and I were at a loss for words. *How could this be*, I wondered. And would it always be this way?

I wished Loren a safe trip home. It would be the last time we would see him for a long time, looking back we are so thankful we had this last dinner and pleasant memory together. There was no way to easily end a thirty-five-year partnership, but we had done it.

*****

The next day, Linda and I drove back to the mine to spend the summer. The miles were difficult as we thought of Loren and our commitment to remain at the mine. Going home would have been much easier than returning as employees rather than owners. We knew it wouldn't be the same.

We arrived at the mine in the evening, and Rabbit and Torr seemed thankful for our return. The next day I was ready to get to work and do my best to help them succeed in their new adventure. I immediately realized Rabbit was willing to listen and learn as much as he could, as quickly as he could. On the other hand, Torr had been watching the placer mining reality shows and thought he had all the answers and knew more than I did. I could see we were in for an interesting summer.

Before Loren left, we had both presented some suggestions on where to start mining on Discovery Creek. Torr had his own ideas, and since he was now the new owner, we went with his plan. Typically, mining is started on a claim, and the operation progresses upstream, establishing drainage for the next cut. The first necessary project was building a road to where we wanted to start mining. Road building is tricky across the permafrost and tundra. Torr began the roadwork and soon learned that you need a good base to build a good road. I had to rebuild what he did, using good bearing soil since he intended to drive a loaded rock truck hauling pay to the wash plant. When the road was finished, we continued stripping and prepared the cut on Discovery to transport pay dirt to the wash plant a mile away on Nansen Creek.

Whenever you open a new mining area there are significant challenges, and our cut was no exception. If you cannot establish drainage, you must set up a pump to dewater the cut, which we did. Rabbit had purchased a rock truck in Whitehorse, and we were ready to haul pay dirt to the wash plant. The sluicing went well on the first cut, and Rabbit and Torr seemed happy and satisfied with what they saw. The first cleanups produced some very nice coarse gold, and you can imagine the excitement in camp.

After mining the first cut, we could see where the gold was. The best pay was on the right limit, and it faded to zero as we mined to the center of the valley. But Torr had other plans.

"Strip further into the deeper left limit," he demanded. I was shocked.

"I'm not doing that," I replied. "That's not where the gold is."

I could see the anger rise in Torr. He was the boss and thought I needed to do what he said, no matter what obvious mistake he was about to make. He gave me the order again, and I looked over at Rabbit. He was clearly in the middle of the disagreement but calmly thinking out the options.

"You can do what he says and come up empty, or do what I say and find gold," I told him. "The best pay is on the right limit. It's fading to nothing going to the left."

Rabbit continued assessing the situation. Finally, he turned to Torr.

"Torr, do what he said," he told him.

I won't recount the next words out of Torr's mouth because they weren't pleasant. Torr was a minor partner in the venture and Rabbit owned ninety percent of the interest, so Rabbit's call was law. Still, Torr wasn't about to be pushed around by a "former" owner. That evening Torr went to Rabbit and told him he wanted me fired and run off the claims. Rabbit realized that Torr's attitude was becoming a liability.

"Brian is staying," Rabbit replied. "You're done here."

Fuming, Torr packed up his things and left while Rabbit and I started a stripping project in an area that we felt would likely have good pay. Three days later, we were in the middle of our workday when we saw somebody approaching with his pickup and trailer. It was Torr coming back to join us again.

Things went more smoothly after that. Rabbit and I spent our time at the wash plant, and Torr loaded the rock truck with pay. When we shut down the sluicing, the crew worked together to clean the box. Rabbit and I did the final gold cleaning, and I was glad to offer many cleanup tips and techniques Loren and I had perfected over the years to recover as much gold as possible.

Rabbit was very good to Linda and me and allowed us time off for an occasional trip to Whitehorse to get away and spend time together. Rabbit even let us use his truck when we picked up supplies for the camp and mine.

Rabbit, his brother-in-law Bob, his friend, Rocky, and I also made a recreational trip to Dawson together. It was a chance for me to introduce him to our gold buyer, who had an office in Dawson City. We spent the weekend seeing the sights and spent an evening at Diamond Tooth Gerties, a famous gambling hall and restaurant. It was a memorable time and a nice getaway from the grind of mining.

When the gold had been refined, the owners were in for a huge disappointment. The reality shows don't tell viewers that placer gold is not one hundred percent pure. Gold mined on Nansen and Discovery Creek assayed at roughly eighty-one percent pure gold. There is fifteen percent silver in the placer gold, and the balance of the weight burns off as melt loss and impurities. When the assay results were in and mailed to Rabbit, he asked me if I thought they were correct. I had tried several times to explain to him placer gold was not pure, and it had a percentage of silver and a small percentage of other impurities, but he never seemed to understand. It is one of the many hard lessons new miners learn when they break into the business.

The rest of the season went as well as expected, but I was disappointed for the new owners. Their gold yield was lower than we expected, and my promised wage cut deeply into the gold they recovered. I will never forget when Rabbit realized what I knew all along.

"You know, the reality TV shows do not show reality," he said. "THIS is reality."

We bid them good luck, and Linda and I loaded our pickup truck and headed to Skagway to take the Alaska Marine Highway to

Bellingham, Washington, and drive back to Nevada.

In the Spring of 2018, Rabbit called me. He asked me to return to Nansen Creek and work with them during the mining season, three weeks on and two weeks off. He also said I could name my wage. I gave the offer serious thought, but ultimately declined. Being at the mine as an employee was difficult for me, and the idea of going through another summer without Loren was still a fresh wound. I didn't relish the idea of making the trip up to the Yukon again and having to file Canadian income taxes for another year. However, the biggest reason to stay home now was Linda. She had been an incredibly good sport throughout our entire mining adventure. It was time to spend our summers together, unencumbered by gold mining.

From the outside, it seemed my mining days were over. My mine was gone. My partnership with Loren was dissolved. Mining would never be the same and I wasn't about to go looking for opportunities. But like so many times before, gold kept finding me.

CHAPTER 12

LIFE FULL CIRCLE

In 2016, the man who first showed me how to prospect with a gold pan more than thirty years earlier called me and asked me to help him with his mine. My cousin, Tim Green, was mining near the old town of Candle, Alaska, on the Seward Peninsula and needed help with his stripping project for the season. Much to Linda's dismay, the call for me to mine again with the family was strong. Tim had three sons—Jacob, Levi, and Adam—who would make up his crew. I don't know how I did it, but I talked Linda into letting me go again. Maybe it helped that I was not asking her to serve as camp cook. Tim's wife, Connie, would do the honors! Candle is an interesting town with a long history in mining. It's a fly-in location for people and supplies. At one time, Candle Creek was rich with placer gold from three bucket line dredges. Today's miners see evidence of drift mining (hand mining) in many areas of the creek, and Tim has used these areas as targets for his prospecting. Records indicate miners have taken 600,000 troy ounces of gold from Candle Creek.

Miners fly in their heavy equipment on Tim's five-thousand-foot landing strip. Tim used a C-130 to get his three excavators to Candle, two Caterpillar 320s, and a Caterpillar 330. It took three trips to fly in his Caterpillar D9R crawler and four trips for his Caterpillar D10N crawler dozer. Tim's claims are patented, so he basically owns the town of Candle and one thousand acres of land in the drainage.

On my first trip to Candle, I took an Alaska Airlines flight to Kotzebue and hired a local air service to fly me eighty miles from

Kotzebue to Candle in a Cessna 206. The price for the one-way trip was $600, which was typical in Alaska. Tim was disgusted with the price and also that the pilot told me to take a seat in the back "like a piece of luggage." Tim was a pilot and open to buying his own plane if the claims were rich enough to justify the investment.

We spent three weeks stripping a deep cut on what is known as Bull Hill. The cut was a disappointment, and Tim looked for more shallow ground to recover his losses. It was also a difficult season for his sons. Tim was pushing them hard, and they didn't like the mining life as much as they thought they would. They did return with Tim in 2018, but I did not since it took a while for him to recover after the disappointing 2016 season.

I knew mining without Loren would be lonely and different, and it certainly was. Since the selling of the mine, our relationship remained strained. Our conversations were necessary, limited, and strictly business as we finalized our Yukon affairs. It's not that there were any particularly hard feelings; we were just busy. Also, without the mine to talk about, we didn't know where to start. In a way, it was just easier not to talk. Our wives didn't reach out to each other either. Maybe we were enjoying our distance from each other after such an intense time together.

Once Loren and I tied up our loose ends, we didn't talk again until April 2019. I was in Fairbanks, on my way to Candle to help Tim for a few weeks, when my sister Brenda called.

"Brian, did you know Loren is scheduled for heart surgery?" she asked.

I was shocked because I had not heard. I called Loren right away. He was surprised, but glad to hear from me. He told me about the serious surgery he was facing, which was a quadruple bypass. Loren told me he had waited until he was 65 and on Medicare to get the surgery, which may have been a mistake. As we were saying goodbye, I knew it was the right time to say something to him I hadn't told him in decades.

"I love you, Loren."

"I love you too, Brian," he answered.

I hung up the phone, a mixed bag of emotions. I was worried, yet happy and relieved that we were connected again. No matter what happened, Loren was going into the surgery knowing our relationship and the feelings we had for each other had survived the break-up of the business.

The surgery was rough. The surgeon couldn't do the fourth bypass because of the condition of Loren's veins. They revived Loren twice on the operating table. He returned home but was never the same again. He struggled with his recovery because he was a man used to working hard, which was impossible in his current state. The entire situation was frustrating for him.

On Christmas Eve of 2019, we were at our condo in Puerto Vallarta when I decided to call Loren. He didn't answer but called me back on Christmas Day and told me he was going in for some medical tests. He was concerned that it might be cancer. My best Christmas gift of 2019 was that call with Loren. It was a turning point where we broke the ice and reset our relationship as loving brothers instead of tense business associates. We had an hour-long conversation about his health and family. More conversations followed between Christmas and the spring of the following year, catching up and becoming best friends again. When Loren heard about me planning to return to Candle, he was impressed.

"I don't know how you do it," he said.

In January, we found out that Loren had lung cancer. It was large cell lung cancer, but treatable. I called Loren, and I could tell he was optimistic. He had a plan to beat it, including chemotherapy. However, everyone was concerned because his heart was so weak. We spoke regularly then, perhaps every ten days or so. I know Deed was taking good care of him, and he was doing as well as he could under the circumstances. A few months later, he told me the cancer had spread to his liver. After that, we didn't talk about his recovery or treatment plans. We discussed anything else we could.

*****

Transport of goods throughout Alaska can be expensive. In 2018, the cost to deliver freight from Fairbanks to Candle was $2 a pound. That meant if you wanted a $6 gallon of milk and the gallon weighed eight pounds, the cost of the milk would be $16 plus the cost of the milk itself—$22. Tim decided it was time to invest in a twin-engine Piper Navajo for the camp's use. Tim was not yet certified to fly the Navajo, but he had a good friend named Timbre that would fly it for him on nights and weekends.

While Loren was recovering from his heart surgery, I traveled to Candle and spent six weeks helping with the stripping, then returned in the fall for four weeks to help prepare for the 2020 season. Tim hired a couple of young men for the beginning of the summer because his sons could only help later in the season.

Then 2020, the famous year of the pandemic, rolled around. On March 26, 2020, Loren was home in Texas when his blood pressure took a dive. Deed rushed him to the ER, but she could not come in because of the COVID restrictions. They kept him overnight in the ICU, and in typical independent Loren fashion, he got out of bed to go to the bathroom by himself. He collapsed on the floor, code blue. The stress of the entire event had been too much for his heart.

When I got the call from my brother Lowell, Linda and I had just left our condo in Puerto Vallarta and had returned to Nevada. The lockdown was now in place, so traveling to the memorial was out of the question. Only Deed, her children, and granddaughter were at Loren's gravesite.

My heart was broken. Losing Loren was much more than losing a friend; in many ways, he was my better half and the person who was always there for me. I was better with him than without him, and I know he felt the same. Losing him was also palpable on many levels. He was my near twin brother, but his death also meant something significant for our family legacy. He was the third founding member of the original Johnson Mining Company to leave the Earth. I was now the sole survivor.

The reality of losing him was bittersweet. I was so grateful for the serious, heart-to-heart talks we had together after each diagnosis and before his procedures, yet I was also sad that I had lost more than two years with him because of the stress caused by ending our mining venture. I would still smile when I thought of what we often said to each other when we succeeded together.

"We're better than we think we are."

We absolutely were. And without Loren around, it would be a life-long challenge to be as good alone as I was with him.

*****

In 2020, I flew to Candle with a fresh pain in my heart from Loren's passing. I knew it would also be a welcome distraction. Tim wanted me to help with an ambitious deep-stripping project. My original plan was to spend five or six weeks stripping a cut about fifty-five feet deep on Bull Hill.

On the third day I was there, Tim woke up at five o'clock in the morning, doubled over in pain. He texted his pilot, Timbre, who lived in Fairbanks, to bring the Navajo to Candle to transport him to the hospital. Connie accompanied him on the two-hour flight from camp to Fairbanks. Tim was in extreme pain the whole time. About an hour outside Fairbanks, his appendix burst, putting Tim in serious condition.

Connie and Tim were in Fairbanks for two weeks as Tim battled serious infections, including sepsis. By then, COVID-19 was spreading everywhere, even in remote Alaska. The virus complicated Tim's hospital stay, but he avoided getting COVID himself. However, he knew that when he was released, it would be a long time before he could work again at camp.

Meanwhile, I tried to fill Tim's shoes while he was recovering. I ended up staying in Candle for eight weeks, several weeks longer than I planned. I worked with his sons and another hired guy to keep the work going. We were on the equipment late into the evening, trying to complete all the stripping before the warm weather turned the frozen tundra into unmovable muck.

The Bull Hill cut was still disappointing. I returned in the fall for four weeks to help prepare for the 2021 mining season. While I was there, Linda traveled to Palm Desert to see her family. When she returned home to Nevada, she was stricken with COVID. I offered to leave Candle and return home to care for her, but Linda encouraged me to stay.

"You don't want this," she said wearily.

Linda told me her friends were taking good care of her, delivering food, and calling to check in often. When I finally returned home to Nevada, she was eleven days out from the infection and feeling much better. Luckily, she was never hospitalized.

* * * * *

After Loren passed, Linda and I expressed our long-distance condolences to Deed and called her several times. We knew how hard it must have been for her to lose Loren. They were basically joined at the hip! Just before he passed, Loren and Deed had bought a house that needed work. Deed kept herself busy decorating the home just the way she wanted it. One of Deed's great talents was interior decorating. She was very creative, and we used to say she could turn a shack into a palace.

In January 2021, Linda reached out to Deed on a Monday night. She was in good spirits and chatted happily about the changes she had made and how she was down to the last detail—the installation of some beautiful green curtains she was ready to hang. We talked and laughed and had the most carefree conversation we'd had with her in thirty-five years. We discussed life and family, and it was obvious that with Loren gone, we had put all the hard feelings behind us.

Five days later, Deed's daughter Anna, who lived nearby, was trying to contact her mother. She texted her on Friday and didn't hear back, which was unusual. On Saturday morning, she still had not heard from Deed. Anna drove to Deed's house and found her mother on the floor, collapsed from an aneurism, but still alive. Deed was on life support long enough for her son, Michael, to fly in from Madison to see her. She died just five days after we spoke and less than a year since Loren had died. With her passing, I once again felt the weight of Linda and I being the sole survivors of our family mining enterprise. Because of COVID, the family just held a private graveside service, similar to what was done for Loren.

A few months later, I traveled to Candle again for four weeks of stripping with Tim and his crew. Traveling was still dreadful with the continuing COVID-19 situation. I felt that wearing a mask on airplanes was stifling and ineffective in controlling the virus. The stripping went well, and as usual, I was happy to leave for home knowing I had helped prepare Tim for another season of successful mining. I had also showed Tim our trick of cleaning the inside of the jig and processing the built-up dried concentrates. When Tim took apart his jig, it yielded fifty troy ounces of gold! It was an incredible, unexpected bonus to cover some of his startup costs.

In July of 2021, Tim invited me to a halibut fishing trip in Ninilchik, Alaska. Halibut are huge fish that can measure up to eight feet in length. I caught a sixty-pounder, the largest fish of the group on the boat, but it wasn't a record-breaker. Years earlier I had caught a seventy-pound halibut with Tim and his brother. This time, we cut our trip short because of stormy weather and rough water that would prevent us from fishing larger halibut. We would have had to stay in the calmer waters, leaving only the "chickens" for us to catch.

The boat captain and crew cleaned the Halibut and dropped them off to be flash frozen overnight. We picked up our fish in the morning and the six of us returned home with twenty-two and a half pounds of halibut each. Tim dropped me off at the airport and I took the "red eye" to Seattle that night.

*****

Another important event in 2021 occurred on August 28, with the wedding of our daughter, Kelsey, to her fiancé, Chris. They married in Reno with a small ceremony attended by close family friends. We held the reception in our nearby backyard in Sparks. Kelsey's two ten-year-old twin daughters served as her flower girls.

A few days later, I was to fly to Fairbanks and onto Candle the next day. When I arrived in Fairbanks, Linda called and told me that Kelsey, Chris, and their girls had COVID. Knowing I had been exposed during the wedding, I felt I should test before getting on Tim's plane to Candle so I wouldn't expose everyone at camp to the virus. At the time, I was with Walt Nielson, an old friend of mine. He was also Tim's expeditor and made sure everything Tim needed made it to camp. The airport was very quiet because of the pandemic. They were also offering COVID tests, so Walt and I both tested and were grateful that we were both negative. The next afternoon, I boarded Tim's plane and flew to Candle.

I started stripping the cut for 2022 the next day. However, a few days later, I began to feel very weak and tired. At first, I was in denial that anything was wrong with me. I tried to ignore my body, continuing to work as hard as possible. Yet I found myself having to stop the Cat and rest for a few minutes during the day. After another couple of days, I was feeling all the symptoms of the COVID-19 virus. We didn't have tests, but I just knew.

On the sixth night, I didn't sleep and couldn't pull myself out of bed. I was having a difficult time breathing and getting comfortable. Before I realized how sick I was, Connie entered my cabin to change my bedding. After a couple of days, she began to feel sick, too.

I FaceTimed with Linda, and she could see how sick I was. She was especially concerned because of my remote location. With masks and social distance, Timbre flew me to Fairbanks, and I met Linda there to help me recover at an Extended Stay Hotel. We stayed eight days until I felt better and was no longer contagious. It took at least a month before I felt normal again.

It was unfortunate that I brought the virus to the mining camp, and Tim, Connie, and their boys all ended up getting sick. Thankfully, Tim and his family didn't hold it against me, and in some ways, were grateful to get it and have natural immunity to reinfection.

*****

I returned to Candle in April 2022 and planned to stay for three weeks. With Linda's consent, I stayed for four. The weather was perfect for the first three weeks, with temperatures near or below freezing. We were able to get the stripping nearly completed on the large cut. The weather warmed up after the third week, and the spring breakup was in full swing. We were thankful to have Tim's military 6x6 truck, a M939, five-ton designed to transport a 10,000 pounds (4,500 kg) cargo load over all terrain in all weather.

It was a monstrous, powerful vehicle that we thought could handle anything… if we could handle the vehicle!

One morning, I was exiting the truck when my hard-soled shoe slipped off one of the wet footholds on the truck. I was four feet off the ground, and I fell backwards, landing flat on my back! The fall knocked the wind right out of me. I felt as if I had bruised my ribs, and I spent the remainder of my stay in Candle in pain.

Candle Creek meandered through the wilderness, and we worked on both sides. Sometimes, we crossed the creek a dozen times a day to get our work done. It was relatively shallow, so it posed no threat. Then, one day we awoke to a beautiful spring day with warmer than average temperatures. Tim, Levi, Adam, and I piled into the 6x6 and headed to the creek to start work.

When we arrived, we saw that the creek had swelled considerably during the night. Evidently, the warmer temperature had hastened the spring runoff from the nearby mountains and turned our creek into a roiling river. Undeterred, we rolled into the river in 6x6 and started across. Suddenly, the truck began to struggle, mid-stream. The oversized tires were turning but we were sitting still. We had stopped on a patch of ice under the water, and we were stranded in the rising water. Fortunately, the weight of the massive truck prevented us from being carried downstream, but Levi and Adam scurried to secure the cargo in the back. We could see some of it bobbing its way down the creek.

In seconds, water began entering the cab of the truck where

Tim and I were sitting. We raised our legs to stay out of the icy cold water. Luckily, we had a gun with us, and the boys fired three shots in the air, hoping Connie would hear it back at camp. The horn still worked so Tim joined in, honking it frantically.

We waited desperately, eyes trained on the road back to camp in hopes of seeing her. We were only a half mile away. If she heard us, we were confident she would know we were in trouble. After what seemed like an eternity, we spotted Tim's old pickup truck tearing down to the creek towards us. It was Connie. We yelled to her to get the excavator, and she took off in the direction of the equipment. Then we waited. Tim and I tried to stay dry from the river that was now running through our cab. Adam and Levi continued climbing to high ground on the truck bed, also attempting to escape the water's icy grip.

After what seemed like hours, we breathed a sigh of relief as we saw the excavator slowly rolling towards us, Connie at the controls. She walked the excavator into the creek and stretched the bucket towards the truck. Carefully, Levi climbed aboard the bucket and rode back to shore, where his mother gently lowered him to the ground. Then he climbed into the excavator and headed towards us.

Reentering the creek again in the excavator, Levi gently hooked the teeth of the bucket onto the back of the tailgate and gently pulled us back towards the shore. Once our wheels contacted the creek bed, we were able to back out of the water and onto shore.

Once on land, we celebrated for a bit, laughing, and

congratulating ourselves on the excellent team effort in a crisis. Then it was time to see how our equipment survived the ordeal. Miraculously, the systems on the 6x6 were okay. We had a lot to be thankful for!

We worked around camp the next few days on backburner tasks, waiting for the creek to recede. A full week passed before the 6x6 could cross the creek safely. It was unfortunate because in the mining business, wasted time is wasted money.

Later in the season, we decided to fly to Nome for a break and spend a day with our friend Mitch Erickson, my lifelong friend who had traveled up to Birch Creek with me for our first year of mining so long ago. Adam was learning to be a pilot with Tim's help, and we flew there in a Cessna 182. Mitch had spent twenty-two years in Nome, where he raised his family and was also involved in the gold mining business. Mitch gave us a detailed tour of Nome, and at about four o'clock in the afternoon, we decided it was time to return to Candle. We piled into the Cessna, and off we went. However, about thirty minutes into our trip with a headwind, we noticed the fuel gauge begin to drop unexpectedly. We returned to the main airport in Nome to top off the fuel tank. It was the right decision. We traveled 130 miles to Candle and landed safely.

Two days after we returned from Nome, Adam and Levi decided to take the Cessna for a practice flight. After a safety check on the airplane, they took off. Immediately, they noticed gas drips on the instrument panel and then at their feet. They circled back, landed the airplane, and removed the engine cover. They found that the main fuel line was only "finger tight," not tightened as it should have been with the proper tool. The gasoline continued to drip from the bottom of the airplane for more than an hour.

The annual FAA safety inspection had been done just prior to flying the airplane to Candle that spring. Adam estimated he had twenty hours of flying on the plane since that time. We realized how fortunate we were that we didn't have an air emergency that ended in disaster on our trip to Nome or during the flying Adam had been doing around Candle.

* * * * *

April 2023 brought me back to Candle to help Tim and his boys strip for the 2023 mining season. I had been in Puerto Vallarta for the winter and returned to Sparks, Nevada, a few days before catching a flight to Fairbanks on the 23rd of April. Tim arranged to fly me from Fairbanks to Candle the same day so I wouldn't have to spend the night.

On April 28, we had a dusting of snow in camp that covered a dangerous patch of ice between my cabin and the kitchen/dining room. I was aware of the ice and cautiously tried to avoid it on my way to breakfast. However, I took one false step and slipped, crashing my left arm against my rib cage on my left side. There was a slope to the ice, and I felt as if I had been slammed to the ground. I lay on the ice with the wind knocked out of me. I was in terrible pain and tried to crawl off the patch of ice to get back on my feet. I couldn't move, and the pain was excruciating. I looked around and I was all alone. I had my cell phone, so I tried to call and text Tim through the satellite system, but there was no answer. I called Connie and, luckily, she answered and sent Tim outside to help me up. We walked together to breakfast and although I was in pain, I was determined to sit on the bulldozer and get to work ripping and pushing the frozen black muck. I worked all day through the pain like the stubborn Scandinavian I am.

That evening, I slept in the recliner in my cabin all night because lying flat was uncomfortable. The next morning, I felt like I had been run over by a truck. I texted Tim and told him I could not join the stripping crew that day. I figured my ribs were broken because I could feel them popping and shifting. However, I thought I'd be fine after a few days of rest.

Tim brought me breakfast, lunch, and dinner the first three days of my recovery. I was determined to feel better in a few days and return to work. It took two weeks before I thought I could finally help again. After breakfast, the four of us walked up a short incline to the shop area, where my Cat was fueled up and ready for me. I got halfway up the incline and was starving for oxygen. I leaned over and grabbed my knees, trying to breathe. The crew could see my condition, so Adam fetched an ATV to return me to my cabin. I spent the morning there but was determined to join them in the afternoon.

After lunch, I joined them at the mining site and finished out the day. The next day, I took an ATV to the Cat, but I had to catch my breath as I climbed into the seat to warm up the engine. I worked all day, but after dinner I had to come clean to Tim about my condition. "Tim," I said, "I'm very concerned about my ability to breathe."

Tim nodded and immediately contacted Timbre to transport me to Fairbanks. He arrived around eleven o'clock that night, and I climbed into the Navajo and crawled into a rear-facing seat. I buckled in, panting to catch my breath. I couldn't help thinking that if I had trouble breathing at sea level, what would it be like at seven thousand feet? Timbre took off, and I tried to relax and breathe normally. I found it I just held very still; I could breathe okay.

After a few minutes in the air, I caught sight of the beautiful Alaskan midnight sun setting in the northwest. It was like a sign to me, a setting sun on my adventures in Candle. It was also my third health problem at camp, and I was enacting the baseball rule: three strikes and I'm out.

When Timbre and I landed in Fairbanks, Walt Neilson was waiting and drove me to Fairbanks Memorial Hospital. They checked me into the ER, and the X-rays showed I had a broken rib. He also spotted fluid in my chest cavity and suggested I return the next day and have more X-rays to determine if the fluid was dissipating or increasing.

I stayed in Tim's shop apartment that night and returned to the hospital the following day. The doctors told me there was no change in my chest fluid, but the X-rays showed I had broken four ribs. They couldn't do much for me because they don't even wrap ribs anymore; you just have to let them heal. However, I was in so much pain, I couldn't return to Candle. Nor could I get home to Linda.

The next day, I met my good longtime friends, Andrea Gelvin, her brother, Randy Frank, and Randy's wife, Georgianne, for lunch. When Andrea, an EMT, saw me, her pleasant expression turned to one of alarm.

"You don't look like yourself, Brian," Andrea said. "You are going back to the hospital. I'm off work at four, and I'll take you there."

We had a nice lunch together, and true to her word, Andrea took me back to the ER. This time, they told me I had eight broken ribs, and they admitted me to the hospital. The next day, they drained over two liters of fluid from my chest cavity so my lungs would have some room to breathe. I was released after three days and advised not to fly back to Nevada for at least a week. It was the worst pain I ever felt in my life.

* * * * *

Finally, back in Nevada, I slept upright in a recliner for seven weeks. It took months to heal, but I grew steadily stronger. I'm still healing today, months later. My physical struggles reminded me of Loren and how he had tried unsuccessfully to keep up with the mining life through his pain. I feel a little of the emotion he must have felt, knowing his mining days were behind him.

I am officially retired from mining now. I will fill my days with other pursuits, including more travel back to Wisconsin to stay connected with friends and family. Linda and I have also moved outside Phoenix, again lured by many friends who live there and enjoy it. The location will make commuting to Puerto Vallarta easier, and we will be able to spend more time there too.

Not a day goes by that I don't miss Loren, think about him, or see something that triggers a memory. Even through the camp drama, disappointing pay dirt, equipment hassles, and wearying travel, I'm glad we lived the life we did, and I'm glad I could share it with Loren and Linda.

Now that I'm older and wiser, I see that gold is more than the precious minerals we extract from the Earth. Gold is where you find it in the loving relationships that make your life worthwhile. It's also found in the valuable lessons that you learn along the way. Find them and you'll uncover the best treasures of your life.

*****

EPILOGUE

My family, my faith, and mining have taught me many things that have shaped my life and approach to adversity. These "gold nuggets" have brought a treasure of peace and prosperity to my life far beyond material wealth. I want to share them with you now, hoping that doing so will save you decades of gold mining to figure it out yourself!

LISTEN AND RESPOND TO THOSE AROUND YOU.

I often failed to understand how much pressure Loren was under from Deed and respond as I should have. We must listen to those around us and always respond with love and empathy.

TAKE TIME TO ENJOY LIFE.

As much as I loved my work, I look back and see what I sacrificed working my summers away. Sometimes, we must prioritize other things over work—rest, family, leisure, planning, etc.

TO BE YOUR BEST, NEVER STOP LEARNING.

Torr learned the hard way in Chapter 11 that gold mining, as shown on reality TV, was anything but reality, and there was much more to learn. We must continuously learn from our experiences and that of others. Loren and I learned new things every day, and we never stopped learning from the advice of fellow miners.

LOOK FOR TREASURE IN UNEXPECTED PLACES.

Loren and I certainly didn't expect to find gold inside our cleaning jig, but there it was! In most of our lives, there is someplace we have not looked to find what we need, whether it's asking someone for advice, seeking prayer, making a change in your life, etc. Where is the hidden "gold" in your life?

THINK BEFORE YOU DO.

Loren and I learned, "If it's not in your head, it's in your back." It was essential to have a good plan before we started a project. In gold mining, as in life, you won't find the treasure immediately. Decide on a plan and stick to it with patience and perseverance.

FINISH THE JOB WELL BEFORE YOU START ANOTHER.

Our equipment maintenance often taught us that sometimes things are beyond a quick repair, and doing a fast fix will not yield a permanent solution. Loren and I used to say, "There is nothing more permanent than a temporary fix." We tried to take our time and fix things right the first time. You must break it all down and start again. Sometimes, it's often the same for relationships as well.

TO BE SUCCESSFUL, YOU MUST ANTICIPATE PROBLEMS AND MINIMIZE RISK.

In life, business, and mining, knowing your vulnerabilities and preparing your defense against the worst possible scenario is critical. In other words, fortify your retaining ponds against floods and keep an eye on your sluice box! We saw many miners go under because they took too much risk or just had too little experience to protect themselves and their assets.

EXPERIENCE IS A GREAT TEACHER.

Loren and I became good at what we did because we were open to new experiences. We learned a lot from trial and error and could then pass on what we knew to our fellow miners and neighbors to help others succeed.

PEACE AT ANY PRICE IS IMPORTANT IN A SMALL SPACE.

Tim mentioned many times how well I fit into his camp and operation because I'd had years of experience learning to get along in a small community. It takes a flexible personality to live peaceably with others in close circumstances for an extended period. Whether it's a mining camp, a dormitory, or a family in a small home, everyone needs to compromise and be agreeable to solving problems. That's the only way everyone will survive.

and finally…

DON'T BE AFRAID TO FOLLOW YOUR DREAM!

Loren and I had a remarkable partnership and earned a more than comfortable living for our families by doing what we loved. We were raised by entrepreneurs. Living the everyday nine-to-five job was not in our DNA, so we found a way to be content, independent, and financially stable. We chose a different kind of life that was foreign to other people but made sense to us. Don't be afraid to do what feels natural to you.

May you always find the gold in your life, regardless of what you're doing or where you're heading. It's there, shining through. Keep looking!

ABOUT THE AUTHOR

Brian Johnson is a different type of entrepreneur who has taken the road less traveled and lived a life of adventure. Originally from Poplar, Wisconsin, Brian grew up in his family's pulpwood logging business, learning from his father how to make a living off the land. He never regretted his decision to forgo an athletic scholarship and embrace his natural talent operating heavy equipment for construction projects. Brian successfully began mining gold in 1981 in Alaska and later in the Yukon. He has mined almost consecutively for forty years, working alongside his close friend and confidant, his brother Loren, for most of it. Since closing his mine in 2016, he has advised other miners in improving their operations and traveled and worked extensively in Candle, Alaska with his cousin, Tim, on a mining venture there. Brian has shared his mining adventures with his wife, Linda, and daughter, Kelsey. Today, Brian is the sole survivor of the original three family members who started the mining company and lived to tell their tale. Brian and Linda live in Maricopa, Arizona, and winter in Puerto Vallarta, Jalisco, Mexico, where they enjoy the culture of Mexico with Mexican, Canadian, and American friends making their permanent or winter homes there.

Made in the USA
Las Vegas, NV
07 November 2023

80413533R00149